FIRST PRINCIPLES:

OR, THE

ELEMENTS OF THE GOSPEL,

ANALYZED AND DISCUSSED

IN

LETTERS TO AN INQUIRER.

BY ISAAC ERRETT.

CINCINNATI:
H. S. BOSWORTH.
1868.

THE CHRISTIAN STANDARD:

AN EIGHT-PAGE, WEEKLY,

RELIGIOUS FAMILY NEWSPAPER,

PUBLISHED IN CLEVELAND, O.,

Devoted to a Pure Christianity, Family Culture, Science, and Religious Intelligence from all parts of the world.

It is now in its third volume, and growing rapidly into extensive circulation.

TERMS: Two Dollars a year, in advance. Subscriptions received at any time.

As THE STANDARD circulates extensively over thirteen States, it is a capital medium for advertising.

Send money, at our risk, by Express, Money Orders, or in Registered letters.

Address, *ISAAC ERRETT,*
Cleveland, Ohio.

JANUARY 1, 1868.

FIRST PRINCIPLES:

OR,

THE ELEMENTS OF THE GOSPEL,

ANALYZED AND DISCUSSED

IN

LETTERS TO AN INQUIRER.

BY ISAAC ERRETT.

CINCINNATI:
H. S. BOSWORTH.
1868.

INTRODUCTORY NOTE.

The Letters composing this little volume, originally appeared in the editorial columns of the CHRISTIAN STANDARD—a weekly paper, devoted to the advocacy of Primitive Christianity, published in Cleveland, Ohio. At the urgent request of many of the readers of that paper, they are now published in a more permanent form, with the hope that they may redeem many honest inquirers from confusion and doubt, and lead them into a clearer understanding and better appreciation of the scope of the Bible, and of the plan of salvation.

The Letters have undergone a very slight revision—it being thought best to retain the easy and simple epistolary style in which they were originally written.

Already we have received many encouraging assurances of the good accomplished by these Letters. Were it not that we are thus authorized to hope that they may do still larger good in this permanent form, we could not consent to their reappearance. They are affectionately urged on the attention of all anxious inquirers after truth.

ISAAC ERRETT.

CLEVELAND, O., Dec. 17, 1867.

FIRST PRINCIPLES,

OR THE ELEMENTS OF THE GOSPEL.

LETTER FROM AN INQUIRER.—I.

To the Editor of the Christian Standard:

DEAR SIR:—I was glad to learn, from a recent number of your paper, that you propose soon to give your readers a course of essays on what your people call "First Principles." Permit me to express the hope that you will begin soon, and that you will not forget your promise to make them plain and easy to be understood; for I assure you there is great need of plain and simple instruction on these important subjects. I have, perhaps, no right to obtrude on you my own spiritual troubles and perplexities, but it may be a help to many others, troubled in the same way, if I tell you some of my difficulties and thereby direct your pen to their removal.

I am not a professor of religion, not because I am not religiously inclined, but because I cannot see how to get my feet on the rock. I was raised religiously, in the orthodox faith, in one of the straitest of Calvanistic Churches. I was trained to study and revere the Bible, and was made familiar with its contents—especially the Old Testament. The venerable preacher to whom I looked in my boyhood with reverence and awe, as an ambassador of God, preached mostly from the Old Testament, and kept us most of the time at the base of Sinai, affirming that the law is our schoolmaster to bring us to Christ. Now, I confess to you that religion seemed to me a very awful thing, and very mysterious, too; for I never could learn definitely how to become a Christian. I heard much good preaching, but it failed to tell me how to get to Christ; and the whole book has seemed to me to be a strange jumble of mysterious things, without beginning, middle, or end. Then, too, I was taught that regeneration was a miraculous work, which God alone could perfom; and as it has never pleased him to perform this work of grace in me, I am sometimes led to fear that I never can be saved. I therefore try, for my own peace of mind, to banish the subject from my thoughts, but I cannot. It is too great a subject to be easily dismissed. I do not know much of your belief, though I have heard many strange things about it. But a few numbers of the STANDARD, handed me by a friend, have interested me, and I come now to ask for information. If you please, I will, from time to time, state my difficulties, both about the Bible and about your people, as they have been represented to me, and ask for knowledge such as I can rely on.

Please tell me, then: Is it true that the Disciples deny the Old Testament? 2. If so, on what grounds? 3. If not, how can you make anything clear and consistent out of the heterogeneous assemblage of books called the Bible? Is the Gospel in Genesis, and Judges, and Ezekiel, and Romans, and Revelations? How are the mysteries of this strange book to be unlocked?

AN INQUIRER.

LETTER I.

Former testament abrogated.—The last will and testament supersedes all others.

TO AN INQUIRER.

MY DEAR SIR:—I am obliged to you for your frank statement and inquiries. It will give me pleasure to assist you, if possible, to a better comprehension of the plan of salvation, as developed in the Bible. I shall not, perhaps, enter upon the solution of your difficulties with as much appearance of system as you expect to find; but, with an eye to the difficulties of others, as well as those which you mention, I shall hope, in a plain and easy method, to render help to honest and anxious inquirers. You have the fullest liberty to state frankly your objections, with a promise of kind and considerate treatment.

May I ask you, first of all, to read the New Testament more carefully? The very fact of a *new* testament, will, or covenant, should arrest your attention. If a *new* will or covenant is now in force, and the *old* one has passed away, as Paul affirms (Heb. viii. 13), it will be at once apparent to you that *your* fate is not *immediately* involved in the contents of *former* wills or covenants; and that, however interesting or valuable the study of former testaments may be, an understanding of them is not vital to your interests. Not Genesis, nor Judges, nor Ezekiel, can make known to you the will of God *toward you*, if there is a *new* testament. In saying this, we do not *deny* the inspiration of the Old Testament Scriptures, but *affirm* it; for we cannot with propriety talk of a *new* testament as divine, without implying that the *old* testament, which it supersedes, was from the same source. If a man makes two wills, the fact that only the latter is *now* authoritative does not certainly imply that the former was not from the same hand. Paul says: "We know that what the law saith, it saith to them that are under the law." Rom. iii. 19. But to Christians he says: "Ye are not under the law, but under grace." Rom. vi. 15.

Moreover, if there is a *new* testament, and, as Paul says, a testament is only of force after the testator's death (Heb. ix. 16, 17), it is evident that you must not only come away from the Old Testament, but from the four gospels likewise, before you can learn what there is for you in this will. It was not of force until after Jesus died, and rose again; and it passed into the hands of his executors, the twelve apostles, and was by them opened and announced after it had been sealed with his blood, and after the Holy Spirit came down from heaven, to guide them into all truth in announcing and interpreting it. You must learn the will, therefore, either from what the Lord told them he had put in it (Matt. xxviii. 18–20), or from the will itself, as unfolded and announced by these executors, after they received the Spirit (Acts ii).

That the Old Testament is not absolutely necessary to acquaint you with the way of salvation, may be learned from the fact that these apostles went into Gentile lands with the new testament or covenant, and made Christians of thousands who knew nothing about the former testament. Read the book of Acts entire. This was not because the Old Testament was not from God—for when they preached to Jews, who had the Old Testament, they took their Scriptures and preached Jesus to them. But the fact that Gentiles were made Christians by the *Gospel*, without leading them through the Old Testament, proves that the way of salvation can be learned from the Gospel without the Law.

Yet we recognize the inspiration of the Jewish Scriptures, and in our next will endeavor to show you that while they are not *authoritative* with us, they form an essential part of the development of the plan of human redemption.

LETTER II.

Impossibility of revealing, at once, the plan of salvation.—Progressive development necessary.—Introductory Dispensations; their philosophy and design.

In our first letter we called your attention to certain considerations to convince you that the Old Testament was no longer in force; that the will of God for you and for me, and for all now living, is to be sought in the New Testament—in that testament which was not of force until Jesus died and rose again, but which, ever since the executors or "ministers of the New Testament" opened it on the day of Pentecost succeeding the resurrection of Jesus (Acts ii), has been to all nations the will of our Lord and Savior Jesus Christ. At the same time we sought to show that while the facts prove that the *authority* of the Old Testament has ceased, they prove the *inspiration* of the Old Testament writings. We need enter into no labored argument to prove this. Assuming the divine mission of Jesus, his teachings settle the question. He affirmed that "all things must be fulfilled which are written in the law of Moses, and in the prophets, and in the psalms concerning me." Luke xxiv. 44. He thus recognizes the three general divisions under which the Jews comprehended all their Scriptures. The *law* contained the five books of Moses. *The prophets* embraced the writings of the *former prophets*, as they were termed, the books of Joshua, Judges, Samuel, and Kings; and the *latter prophets*, or those which are generally called now the prophetical books, with the exception of Daniel. The *hagiographa*, or holy writings, comprehended Psalms, Proverbs, Job, Canticles, Ruth, Lamentations, Ecclesiastes, Esther, Daniel, Ezra, Nehemiah, and the two books of Chronicles. We say that our Lord in acknowledging these as the Scriptures, out of which his own divine mission was to be proved, asserts their inspiration.

We are aware that your mind is confused at this point; and you are not alone. You will ask, If inspired, why not of authority? They are of authority *as witnesses* of the Christ; but not of authority *as a law* to us.

"Is God, then, capricious—making one set of Scriptures, and then setting them aside—making one testament, and then, like a man who changes his mind, destroying that will, and making a new one that pleases him better?"

Not at all. To rid your mind of confusion, you must learn one important truth—that the development of the plan of human redemption was *gradual—progressive*. The law of *progressive development* seems to pervade the universe. Science reveals it in the physical universe in the structure of worlds. We need not be surprised, therefore, to find it in the moral universe, in the government of rational natures. We may readily conceive the idea of worlds of matter rising into instant perfection, by omnipotent energy; but we cannot understand how mere omnipotence can control *mind* into instant submission. Rational beings must be plied with *motive*—they must be brought themselves to *choose* the right. This is not accomplished by physical force. It must come by conviction, persuasion, conversion. But to take a race which, in the perverted exercise of its freedom, is drifting away from God, into atheism and utter lawlessness, and prepare them to be saved—to come under the control of such a Lord and Savior as Jesus is, was not the work of a day, or a year, or a century. We are sometimes asked: "Why did not Jesus come as soon as man sinned? Why delay for four thousand years? Why set up institutions and laws that must in the end be abrogated? Why cumber the plan of salvation with a testament that has to be taken away as imperfect?" And this we take to be your difficulty. We reply: The fact that God did not instantly reveal a complete plan of salvation, but took four thousand years to develop it, proves that there were difficulties in the way which required a *gradual unfolding* of his purposes. We may not be able fully to enter into the reasons for this. But there are some reasons for it which we may at least partially understand.

1. Men must learn the odiousness and curse of sin, and the ruin which it inevitably works, before they are even willing to be saved from it. This can only be learned by experience—our own experience, or that of others. Time had to be given, therefore, for the accumulation of sinful experiences.

2. Men had to learn that they could not save themselves from sin. This is a hard

lesson. The pride of the human heart does not easily give away. When the prodigal had wasted his substance in riotous living, his pride would not let him return until he had made the most desperate efforts to retrieve his fortunes. Not until he reached the point of utter despair of his own efforts, through a succession of most humiliating failures, was he willing to arise and go to his father. This is but a picture of human nature—of the race. It required time, therefore, for a succession of human experiments in government and religion.

3. A sinful condition of the human soul does not allow of immediate intercourse with God. Sin erects fearful barriers between man and God. God can only reveal himself *at a distance*. It required a patient succession of revelations, therefore, to overcome the ignorance of God into which sin plunged the race, and prepare mankind for a full revelation of the divine nature and character.

These are some of the reasons why the salvation of God was not immediately revealed in its fullness.

Let us seek an illustration. A father has seven sons. They grow rebellious on his hands. He could *force* them into instant subjection, but that would not suit his purpose. He recognizes the rational nature they possess, and knows that they cannot attain the true dignity of their being, so as to possess a worthy manhood, unless they are *persuaded* to be good. He will not then employ force, except as corrective, until all other means have failed, and they become hopelessly incorrigible. *Then* he may be compelled to cast them off entirely. Meanwhile he seeks to govern them firmly, but kindly; bearing with their perverseness, rewarding them for obedience, and punishing them with more or less severity, as he finds necessary for his authority and their good. Still his kindness is spurned, and his authority contemned. His boys, as they grow up, become more restive under authority, and more stubbornly bent on pursuing their own ways. There is one expedient left: *set them adrift; throw them on their own resources.* They will learn, perhaps, in the school of experience, lessons dearly bought, but which they will learn in no other way. Nothing but experience, it is evident, will take the conceit out of them. So he lets them go every one his own way. But as he has ulterior purposes of grace in letting them go—as he means to hold himself in readiness to receive them when they shall desire to return—he does not entirely abandon them even now. He retains *one* at home and makes him the depository of his counsels, and the recipient of peculiar favors, that through him he may still be able to operate indirectly on the absent prodigals, and hold them by the invisible chain of his providence until the "fullness of time" for their penitential restoration. They are all equally guilty, and his election of any one over the rest to fill this place in his own house is purely a matter of grace. He chooses the one who will best suit his purpose, appoints him his patrimony, and establishes with him paternal relations of peculiar tenderness, while the rest are away on their wild career of experiment. But he elects him not for his own sake merely, *but for the sake of the lost sons*, that they through him may yet be brought back. Thus in all their wanderings they are still watched, and often influenced unknown to themselves. Even the son who stays at home is borne with in many wrongs, for the sake of his influence over them. And when the time comes that they are weary of their vain experiments, and begin to think of returning to their father's house, he is ready through this son to communicate his willingness to receive them, and reinstate them in his favor.

Let the first part of this illustration answer for God's dealings with our race during the first two thousand years, during what is called the patriarchal age. Then, when the nations "did not like to retain God in their knowledge, he gave them up to a reprobate mind," and abandoned them to their own devices. But he chose Abraham and the nation springing from him through Isaac and Jacob, to *stay at home*, and be to him a peculiar people above all people on the face of the earth. He made a testament or covenant for them, *but not for their own sakes:* it was for the sake of the prodigal children who had gone from home, that through this nation he might keep watch and ward over them for their final reconciliation. These nations experimented in government, philosophy, and religion for two thousand years, and failure was heaped on failure until footsore in their wanderings, and heart-sick in their failures—all their substance wasted in riotous living—they began to think of their Father's house, and were ready to listen to overtures. *Then,* "in the fullness of time," Jesus came, and the Gospel was published to the nations.

That the Jewish nation served this purpose, and that they were elected to their position with a view to accomplish such a purpose, is evident from numerous Scriptures. Their location in a geographical center, whence light could successfully radiate—their slavery in Egypt, the center of learning and of idolatry—their connection with Tyre and Sidon, and other great sources of commercial influence—their captivity in Babylon, and their dispersion among the nations, are among the prominent facts that indicate the ulterior purposes of Jehovah in making them his own people, and giving them his law and counsel. See Ex. ix, 16, and xv, 13–17; xxxii, 11–13; Josh. ii, 9–11, and the books of Ezra, Nehemiah, and Daniel. All the nations formed a school, rebellious though they were; and the Jews were the black-board on which God wrote his lessons and wrought out his problems.

Hence, in this progressive development we have three successive dispensations:

1. Patriarchal,	1. The Family,	1. Domestic,	1. Theophany,
2. Jewish,	2. The State,	2. National,	2. Laws.
3. Christian.	3. The Church.	3. Ecumenical.	3. Gospel.

The first period was marked by a vindication of *the Being and Providence of God*, in opposition to the Atheism into which the posterity of Cain were drifting. He that comes to God must believe that He is, and that he is a rewarder of them that diligently seek him. Its revelations were in personal manifestations of Deity and in special rewards and punishments.

The second was marked by a vindication of the *unity* of God, in opposition to the idolatries into which the nations were wandering. Its revelations unfolded the truth, justice, and holiness of the one living and true God.

The third was marked by the *incarnation*—the vindication of Jesus as the Son of God, in opposition to all human schemes of salvation and all human lordship over the soul of man. Its revelations unfold the condescension, mercy, and love of God in Christ. Thus we have God revealed,

1. In special appearances—Theophany.	1. Providence.	1. God in the Family.
2. In Words.	2. Law.	2. God in the Nation.
3. In Flesh—Immanuel—God with us.	3. Grace.	3. God in Humanity —*for the race.*

"The law (*the type*) came by Moses, the grace and the truth (*reality*) came by Jesus Christ." Jno. i, 17. We reach the summit of these purposes when we hear Jesus announcing—"All authority is given unto me in heaven and in earth. Go, therefore, disciple the nations, baptizing them into the name of the Father, and of the Son, and of the Holy Spirit."

LETTER III.

Meaning of the Old Testament only fully learned from the Christian stand-point.—Philosophy of Types.—Uses of the Old Testament to the Christian.

Did you ever visit a printing office? If so, you have been impressed with the fact that the "art preservative of all arts" has, to the uninitiated, many mysteries. As you looked on the types scattered with rapid hand, here and there, in various boxes, apparently without regard to order—then "set up" in the composing stick—transferred to galleys—"made up" in the "form"—and "locked up" in the "chase," ready for the pressman—you could scarcely catch a gleam of intelligence as to the mode by which thought is made visible on paper. Perhaps, looking over the form when made up, you might gather from the cuts and the headings and the catch-lines some faint outline of the leading thoughts meant to be conveyed. But if you undertook to read the intelligence through the types, you would find it a very difficult task. But when the types make their impression on paper, and you see the *antitypes* on the printed sheet, you read without difficulty. You learn that in all the apparent confusion and mystery of type-setting, intelligent mind has been marshaling the types into order, according to "copy," so that the printed sheet exhibits the very thoughts and words contained in the copy that lay before the printer on his case. No blind chance could have brought the types together thus into an orderly arrangement, so as to make words, sentences, paragraphs, and complete essays. Their intelligent utterances prove that they were arranged by *design*—by intelligence working according to pattern or "copy" placed in the compositor's hands.

Equally confused and mysterious to you is the Old Testament. Moses was, so to speak, a printer. God furnished him a fount of type, and gave him "copy." "See that thou make all things according to the pattern shown to thee in the mount." Ex. xxxv, 40. Moses set up the tabernacle and the Jewish worship according to copy. But you cannot read it, except in dim outline—here and there a heading or a picture furnishing an obscure idea of what is intended. But in the New Testament—the Gospel—the impression is *worked off*, as the printers say; and you have *the antitype*, which, like the printed sheet, is plain reading. You must view the Old Testament, therefore, from the Christian stand-point, and all is clear. The Old Testament is a system of types, figures, symbols. It is *pictorial* religion, adapted to the childhood of the race. It presented to the eye, in symbol, the outlines of the great truths of redemption, and in its typical worship familiarized the minds of men with the ideas of sin, of sacrifice, of pardon, of righteousness and sanctification, of rewards and punishments; but in such an imperfect way as to leave the constant impression of incompleteness, accompanied with the promise of better things to come. Thus, as Paul says, (Gal. iii, 24,) "The law was (not *is*) our schoolmaster (*paidagogos*), to bring us unto Christ." The pedagogue was the *child-tender*, to whom children were committed to be led to exercise, to be conducted to and from school, to be superintended, and sometimes to be taught some of their first lessons. Such offices did the law perform dealing with men in a state of tutelage; but, adds Paul, "now that faith has come, *we are no longer under a pedagogue.*" The law was introduced for certain purposes, "until the promised seed (the Messiah) should come."

From all that has been said in this and the former communications, we gather up the main designs of the former dispensations, and learn the uses of the Old Testament Scriptures.

1. They contain a historic development

of the purpose of God to redeem a sinful race. Here we learn the kingdom of God to be, according to the Savior's teaching, of gradual development. "First the blade, then the ear, after that the full corn in the ear." Mark iv. 28.

2. They present a record of the *moral government of the world*—showing how the events of time were strung on a single thread that stretched along the ages: that thread was the purpose of God to prepare the race for the coming of the Redeemer. The rise and fall of kingdoms and empires, as well as the election and reprobation of individuals; and the captivities of the tribes of Israel and Judah, as well as their establishment in the land of Judea, were all arranged and overruled for this one purpose.

3. They reveal the will of God, as addressed to patriarchs and Jews—not his will in reference to us.

4. They contain the types and prophecies of the coming salvation; and are, therefore, a great store-house of evidence for the divinity of the New Testament, for they hold, locked up in permanent forms, the types of Gospel truth and Gospel blessings. "Christ is the *end* of the law to the believer." "The testimony of Jesus is the spirit of prophecy."

5. As moral principles are immutable and eternal, it follows that many most valuable and precious lessons of truth, righteousness, and piety stand on the pages of the Old

Testament, which are of equal application to persons under all dispensations. Hence, "the things that were written aforetime were written for our learning, that we, through patience and comfort of the Scriptures, might have hope." Rom. xv. 4.

6. Its developments of human nature and character are of priceless value. The severe and terrible truthfulness with which the Holy Spirit records the lives of men and women—the virtues of the bad and the vices of the good being alike daguerreotyped in the light of truth, without apology, defense, explanation, encomium, or even exclamation—render it the only genuine gallery of portraits of human character. No uninspired biographies or autobiographies can stand in comparison. The awful, but divine, impartiality of perfect truth, renders the Old Testament, merely as a record of human nature, entirely unique and invaluable.

But a book of authority, to teach *us* what to do, it is not. The Gospel is not found in it, except in type and promise—precisely the forms in which it cannot have authority. The spirit, genius, laws, ordinances, promises, and threatenings of the Gospel are not found on its pages, except as an adumbrative and preparatory system contains in it the germs of all that is afterward to burst into full life. The pedagogue performed his full office—not in teaching the world salvation—but in leading the world to Christ for salvation. The very last injunction in the Old Testament is: "Remember ye the *law of Moses*, my servant, which I commanded him in Horeb *for all Israel*, with the statutes and judgments." Mal. iv. 4. It was the law of *Moses*—not of CHRIST; for *all Israel*—not for *all nations.*

In closing this number I must anticipate an objection which will probably rise in your mind. If God is perfect, and all his works are perfect, how could he be the author of an imperfect system? Does it not derogate from the honor and perfection of Deity to speak of a system of his own devising as "inferior," "imperfect," "shadowy," etc.? Every thing that God creates is perfect *for its own ends.* The night is as perfect as the day, for its own uses; but we do not dishonor God by calling the one darkness and the other light. The moon is as perfect as the sun; but it is no dishonor to God to say that the sun is brighter than the moon. The child is as perfect, it may be, as the man; but it is perfect *as a child.* It is no dishonor to the child to say that the man is larger, stronger, wiser. So was the law perfect *as a pedagogue*, as a *moon*, as a *type.* For its own use it was perfect. But its object was not to teach the way of salvation, nor to give life. And we do the law no dishonor when we say that the Gospel is a better revelation,—that the "new testament" has a "better mediator,' contains "better promises," and is indeed a "better covenant."

LETTER IV.

Classification of the books of the New Testament.

Having glanced at the Old Testament writings, and hastily traced the progressive development of the divine purpose in the redemption of our race, we have learned enough to establish us in the conviction that those writings do not contain a law for us—that their authority has passed away. The same God who at sundry times and in divers manners spoke to the fathers by the prophets, has, in these last days, spoken to us by His Son. We come then, to what is called the New Testament. And you ask, if this is, from first to last, a book of authority; and if we may find everywhere in its pages a knowledge of salvation and of duty? We are compelled to answer, No. What is called the New Testament, is made up, as you are aware, of a number of documents, written at different times, by different persons, with different objects in view. There is no difficulty in reaching this conclusion. A careful reading of the documents will enable any one of ordinary intelligence to classify them in such a way as to give a proper order of succession to the different writings, and a character of completeness to the whole.

1. He will find four biographies, written by different authors, and to different classes of persons, but all having the same definite object in view—to exhibit the incarnation, life, character, and mission of the Son of God, the Savior of men. They embrace what is necessary to be known of Jesus, from his birth to his resurrection and ascension. They are written with the avowed object of *furnishing the materials of a life-giving faith in the Son of God.* "These are written that you might believe that Jesus is the Christ, the Son of God, and that, believing, you might have life through his name." John xx. 51. These records wind up with a revelation of the grand purpose of the mission of Jesus, *to furnish salvation for the race;* and an announcement of a coming Spirit of Truth, under whose guidance chosen men should bear the offer of this salvation to all the world.

2. He will find a succeeding book of history called Acts of the Apostles, taking up the narrative of events where the first four books left it, and proceeding to give a history of the preaching of the Gospel and its results:—a narrative of this salvation offered and accepted—showing how sinners were converted into Christians, being saved from their sins and brought into the Church of Christ. This is to you, let me say, in your present condition, the most important book in the Bible. It shows the Gospel, as

preached to Jews, Samaritans, Gentiles; to kings, princes, nobles, philosophers, religionists, infidels, slaves, and barbarians; to good and bad, rich and poor, learned and ignorant. It may surprise you to find that the original, inspired preachers of the Gospel, did not keep their hearers at the base of Sinai, where you have been for a life-time deafened by the thunders of the law; and that they never said one word about regeneration being a miracle; in fact that there is not one sermon, in all that are reported, *about* regeneration! But you will find here precisely how the Gospel was preached, and how the guilty were led to the fountain of mercy for salvation.

3. He will find a cluster of epistles, addressed *to saved persons*—to *Christians*, to give them a knowledge of the duties, dangers, trials, and hopes, of Christian life: epistles which correct the errors, and reveal the perils, of the Christians; give the instruction, and unfold the motives, necessary to furnish him to all good works.

4. He will find a book of peculiar and imposing symbols, largely concealing and partially revealing the fortunes of the Church through successive ages—symbols meant alike to conceal and to reveal—a kind of *dark lantern* to be carried by the Christian pilgrim, throwing no light out to the world, but to be used as occasion serves, by the believer, to throw light ahead on his path-

way, and cheer him with the coming triumph and glory.

So, then, we have this classification of the New Testament writings:

1. Biographical.	2. Historical.	3. Epistolary.	4. Prophetical.
1. Christ in person.	2. Christ in the Gospel.	3. Christ in his people.	4. Christ in Providence.
1. Christ as the Apostle of the Father, working out a scheme of salvation.	2. Christ as Lord and Savior tendering a perfect salvation to the sinful.	3. Christ as Head of the Church reigning in and over his people.	4. Christ as Sovereign over all things, controlling the events of the ages for the final triumph of his truth.

So that we go to the four Gospels to learn of the Savior; to the Acts, to learn how to be saved; to the Epistles, to learn how the saved ought to live; and to the Apocalypse, to learn the fortunes of the Church and the destiny of its faithful members.

In our next communication we wish to speak more particularly of the first four books of the New Testament.

LETTER V.

Design of the Biographical books—Matthew, Mark, Luke, and John.

In the last letter we gave a classification of the writings of the New Testament, the object of which was to show that the documents contained in that volume were not all written for the same purpose. This is of more importance than, at first sight, it may seem to be. It was only the other day we read an editorial in one of our exchanges designed to prove that baptism is not for the remission of sins. The editor quoted, with a triumphant air, the following Scripture: "If we confess our sins, he is faithful and just to forgive us our sins, and to cleanse us from all unrighteousness." 1 John i. 9. We remember having read the same answer to the inquiry of an anxious sinner on a placard issued by the Young Men's Christian Association of Detroit, and posted up at the entrance of their rooms. Now when you reflect that John's first epistle was not addressed to the unconverted, but to Christians, and that he is stating to Christians how *they* may obtain forgiveness, you will at once see the deception practiced in such an application of this Scripture. With equal propriety might we apply to Christians the language of Peter to a throng of rebel suppliants for mercy: "Repent and be baptized, every one of you, in the name of Jesus Christ, for remission of sins." But the editor aforesaid, not content with one misapplication, sought to fortify his false position by another Scripture. "If thou shalt confess with thy mouth the Lord Jesus, and believe in thy heart that God raised him from the dead, thou shalt be saved. For with the heart man believeth unto righteousness, and with the mouth confession is made unto salvation." Rom. x. 9, 10. Now this language, although occurring in an epistle addressed to Christians, is evidently meant to express the condition of salvation offered to a sinful world. This the context clearly shows. But the perversion here consists in making the penitent *sinner's* confession of *the Lord Jesus* equivalent to the penitent *Christian's* confession *of his sins*. So you see how important it is to note *to whom* the Scriptures are addressed, and *for what purpose* any passage that may be under consideration, was written.

We have already shown that the Old Testament does not contain an authoritative announcement of the Gospel. We now call your attention to the fact that the four Gospels of Matthew, Mark, Luke, and John, were not written as an authoritative announcement of the terms of salvation. They reveal the *Savior* rather than the salvation —what He did to bring salvation to us, rather than what we are to do to make the salvation ours. True, before these records close, the terms of salvation are announced —but it is not *the* design—the main scope—of the writings to treat of these. They furnish, as before stated, the material of a life-giving faith. They make known to us the Savior. They reveal his character and his work. They make us familiar alike with his teachings and example, and give us a broad and firm basis for faith, hope, and love, in a knowledge of his human sympathy and his divine power, his labors of love, his sacrifice for sin, his resurrection from the dead, and ascension to glory. Hence Luke sets forth his design in writing to be, "that thou mightest know the certainty of those things wherein thou hast been instructed," concerning Jesus Christ.

But all this while, the *law of Moses* remains in force. Let us call your attention to a few significant facts, which it is important to keep in mind, in the study of these four books.

1. Jesus was a Jew, "born under the law," and subject to the law. He did not allow his own work to do dishonor, in any way, to the living authority of the law of Moses. He came not to *destroy* the law and the prophets, but to *fulfill*. Matt. v. 17, 18.

2. He taught his disciples to observe the law, and receive the instructions of its authorized expounders. "The Scribes and the Pharisees sit in Moses' seat. All, therefore, whatsoever they bid you observe, that observe and do." Matt. xxiii. 2, 3.

3. His own personal mission was to the Jews only. Matt. xv. 24.

4. The twelve and the seventy whom he sent out, were limited to the Jews in their mission. Matt. x. 5. Luke x. 1.

5. When Moses and Elijah—the great lawgiver and law-restorer—laid down their honors at his feet, and the voice of the Father announced the transfer of authority to Jesus, saying: "This is my beloved Son, *hear ye Him*"—those who were cognizant of the fact

were forbidden to make it known until after the resurrection of Jesus from the dead. See Matt. xvii. 1–9. It is most evident, therefore, that the authority of Moses was not to cease, and the authority of the Messiah was not to be proclaimed, until after his resurrection.

6. He taught his disciples that he must *go away* to *receive* his kingdom. Luke xix. 12.

7. His church was not yet established. Matt. xvi. 18.

8. It was *after* his resurrection that he claimed "all authority in heaven and earth." Matt. xxviii. 18. But he forbade the assertion or annunciation of that authority until he should ascend to heaven and send down the Holy Spirit to guide his apostles into all truth. Luke xxiv. 49. John xvi. 13.

We cannot avoid the conclusion, therefore, that the terms of salvation through Jesus Christ, have yet to be announced with authority. The succeeding book of Acts will inform us of this announcement.

It remains to be said, that these four Gospels are of the most vital importance to us. They reveal the Savior himself, and present to us the divine foundation of faith and hope. Here is "God manifest in the flesh;" no longer hidden in a pavilion of darkness, with a benighted world groping vainly after him; nor proclaiming his presence in earthquake and tempest, and thunder and lightning, as at Sinai—"the great and the dreadful God;" but dwelling among us in the tabernacle of our own humanity—in us and of us; looking out upon us with human eyes, ministering to us with a human hand, weeping human tears in sorrow and sympathy over our woes, binding up our wounds, healing our diseases, with human lips speaking counsels of heavenly wisdom and grace, and bearing our nature in his arms of divinity through all its conflicts, sorrows, and tribulations, nay, even through the helplessness of death, to final triumph and immortal bliss!

Here are the *demonstrations* of God's power and willingness to save. We need no longer doubt either his love or his ability—we need no longer remain ignorant of his gracious design in behalf of our guilty and dying race. Here is the great Sacrifice—the Lamb of God bearing away the sins of the world. Here are the culminations alike of love and of justice, in the voluntary death, for our sins, of the Sinless One, "that whosoever believeth in him might not perish, but have everlasting life." Here is, also, the destruction of death's awful dominion, and the upspringing of life from the grave. Life and immortality are brought clearly to light.

Ah! my dear sir; you may have doubts about human theories of regeneration, and be confused by the contradictory teachings of sects in theology; but can you not understand Jesus Christ? Rather, can you, with an honest heart, fail to understand him?

Do you doubt that he is the Son of God—that he has life in himself—that he gave his life for you—that he is stronger than death—that he lives in heaven a Prince and a Savior, to grant repentance and remission of sins? Do you not *love* him? Has your heart never been touched by his gentle words of pity and mercy? Has he sorrowed, and toiled, and wept, and died, in vain? Do not his tears and blood plead mightily with you? Have not his searching words of counsel and reproof convicted you of sin, made you ashamed of your transgressions? And when he has shown you a father, with open arms, running to embrace with love the returning prodigal, have you not felt that you, too, could say, "I will arise and go to my Father?" And yet you have been waiting for a miracle to regenerate you! Rest assured, that if you believe in the Son of God, and for his sake can turn away from sin and rebellion, and make it your pleasure to do his will, you may be at once admitted to the full joys of his salvation. We are to receive Jesus, believe in Jesus, love Jesus, serve Jesus—not a theoretical, philosophical, or theological Jesus, but the living, personal, loving, holy Jesus, of the New Testament; and all the regeneration the heart can know is in being led to receive his teachings, trust his sacrifice, accept his authority, and enjoy the purifying and ennobling influences of his love. "I am come a light into the world, that whosoever believeth in me might not abide in darkness, but have the light of life." "If a man love me he will keep my words; and my Father will love him; and we will come to him, and make our abode with him." Thus all the treasures of saving grace and redeeming love come to us through *faith* and *obedience.* We have settled the greatest question of life when we have decided that Jesus is able to save and worthy to rule us. It but remains to learn what He would have us do, and heartily accept and obey it. The four Gospels settle the first point. The Acts of the Apostles will guide us to the second.—Before we leave the *testimonies* of Matthew, Mark, Luke, and John—for *testimonies* they are, to be *believed*, not *laws* to be *obeyed; facts* and *principles* to enlighten us concerning the coming kingdom, and not *statutes* and *ordinances* to regulate Christian life—we must invite you to consider the different *missions* which these books unfold.

1. The mission of John the Baptist. 2. The mission of Jesus. 3. The mission of the Twelve. 4. The mission of the Seventy. 5. The mission of the Holy Spirit. 6. The mission of the Apostles. These six missions are all unfolded to view in these four books. A proper comprehension of them will do much to prepare us to understand the gospel of salvation.

There are three questions concerning all these missionaries (for a missionary is one *sent* upon a mission) which it is necessary to ask:

I. *By* whom sent?

II. *To* whom sent?

III. *For what purpose* sent?

Let us briefly consider these questions in reference to these different missions.

I.—John the Baptist.

1. By whom was he sent? Ans. "There was a man sent from God, whose name was John." John i. 6.

2. *To* whom was he sent? Ans. "Behold I send *you* (Jews) Elijah the prophet." Mal. iv. 5. See also Matt. xvii. 12, 13.

3. *For what purpose* sent? Ans. To prepare the way of the Lord, by turning the hearts of the fathers to the children, and the hearts of the children to the fathers; to proclaim the coming kingdom, and to introduce the king. See Mal. iv. 6. Matt. iii. 1–3. John i. 29–34; and iii. 25–33.

Not *here*, then, do we find a mission, world-embracing, in which *our* salvation is apprehensible. The mission of Jesus is a preparatory work.

II. Jesus of Nazareth.

1. *By* whom sent? Ans. The "Father hath sent me." John v. 36.

2. *To* whom sent? Ans. "I am not sent but unto the lost sheep of the house of Israel." Matt. xv. 24.

3. *For what purpose* sent? Ans. "I am come a light into the world, that he that

believeth in me may not abide in darkness." John xii. 46. "The Son of man is come to seek and to save the lost." Luke xix. 10. "To this end was I born, and for this purpose came I into the world, that I might bear witness unto the truth." John xviii. 37. "He shall save his people from their sins." Matt. i. 21.

As we are not Jews, this personal mission of Jesus was not to us. It is still a preparatory work.

III. The Twelve in their First Mission, and the Seventy.

1. *By* whom sent? Ans. "Behold *I* send you," said Jesus. Matt. x. 16. Luke x. 3.

2. *To* whom sent? Ans. "Go not into the way of the Gentiles, and into any city of the Samaritans enter ye not. But go rather to the lost sheep of the house of Israel." Matt. x. 5, 6. Luke x. 1.

3. *For what purpose* sent? Ans. "As you go, preach, saying, The kingdom of heaven is at hand." Matt. x. 7. Luke x. 9.

Evidently this, too, is a preparatory work.

IV. The Holy Spirit.

1. *By* whom was this Divine Missionary sent? Ans. "But the Advocate, which is the Holy Spirit, whom the Father will send in my name." John xiv. 26; xvi. 7.

2. *To* whom sent? Ans. *To the Apostles.* "Whom the world cannot receive." John xiv. 17. "I will send him unto you." [Apostles.] John xvi. 7.

3. *For what purpose* sent? Ans. "When he is come [to you my apostles] he will convince the world of sin, of righteousness and of judgment." John xvi. 8. "He will guide you [apostles] into all truth," verse 8. "He shall glorify me, for he shall receive of mine, and shall show it unto you," verse 9.

Now as the "world cannot receive" this Spirit, and as the promise is to send the Spirit to the Apostles, and not to the world, that the world, *through the apostles*, might be convinced of sin, righteousness, and judgment, it is evident that sinners are not immediately interested in *this* mission. It, too, is preparatory. We come then, lastly, to

V. The Second Mission of the Twelve.

1. *By* whom sent? Jesus says, "All authority in heaven and earth is given to me. Go ye, therefore." Matt. xxviii. 18, 19.

2. *To* whom sent? Ans. "All nations." Matt. xxviii. 19. "All the world—every creature." Mark xvi. 15.

3. *For what purpose* sent? Ans. "Preach the gospel to every creature." Mark xvi. 15. "Disciple all nations, baptizing them into the name of the Father, and of the Son, and of the Holy Spirit. Teaching them to observe all things whatsoever I have commanded you: and, lo, I am with you always, even unto the end of the world." Matt. xxviii. 18–20. "Repentance and remission of sins shall be preached in my name, among all nations, beginning at Jerusalem. And

ye are witnesses of these things. But tarry ye in the city of Jerusalem, until ye be endowed with power from on high." Luke xxiv. 47, 48. "Receive ye the Holy Spirit. Whose soever sins ye remit, they are remitted unto them; and whose soever sins ye retain, they are retained." John xx. 22, 23. "I give unto you the keys of the kingdom of heaven; and whatsoever thou shalt bind on earth, shall be bound in heaven, and whatsoever thou shalt loose on earth shall be loosed in heaven." Matt. xvi. 19.

Here, then, is a mission which *does* immediately concern us; for it embraces "all the world"—"every creature," down to the "end of the world." It is a mission which has salvation in it—the remission of sins; and "all things" which saved people are to be taught to do. It has the HOLY SPIRIT in it—for the Spirit is promised to the apostles to guide their preaching and teaching. It has CHRIST in it;—for the gospel of Christ is put in their keeping, and the Spirit is promised to take the things of Christ and show unto them. It has all of the Old Testament in it that concerns our salvation; for the Lord "opened their understandings, that they might understand the [Jewish] scriptures, to prepare them to preach the Gospel." Luke xxiv. 45–48. So that all of the Old Testament and of Christ, and of the Holy Spirit, needful for our conversion and salvation, is comprehended in this mission of the

apostles. It wants but the coming of the Holy Spirit to guide them into all truth,—and then we shall have found our point of rest; we can sit at their feet and learn the way of salvation.

LETTER VI.

Acts of Apostles—Day of Pentecost.

We have traced the progressive developments of the purposes of God through the Patriarchal and Jewish dispensations. We have watched the finger-boards along the way, all pointing forward to something better yet to be revealed. We have sought an answer to the question, "Wherefore, then, serveth the law?" and have, we trust, at least to some extent, recovered your mind from confusion as to the design and purpose of the Old Testament. We have also become acquainted with the object of the four narratives of Matthew, Mark, Luke, and John, and have seen John the Baptist, Jesus, the Twelve, and the Seventy, all pointing forward to a coming kingdom, not far in the future, whose treasures of salvation should be unlocked to a perishing world as soon as Jesus should receive his authority, and the Holy Spirit should descend from heaven to endow the chosen ambassadors for their glorious mission. The last charge of the Lord to his apostles was, "Tarry ye in Jerusalem until ye be endued with power from on high." Acts i. 1–5.

This brings us to *the day of Pentecost* and its most significant developments, as narrated in the second chapter of the Acts of the Apostles. Here we reach our point of rest. Here is the grand culmination of the scheme of salvation. Here is the setting up of the kingdom. Here is seen "the little stone cut out of the mountain without hands," which Nebuchadnezzar saw, and which is yet to become a great mountain and fill the whole earth. Here is the "fullness of the blessing of the Gospel of Christ."

We may well afford to linger here a little while, and survey the sacred ground, and endeavor to take in the greatness and grandeur of the events which here transpired on that memorable day of Pentecost.

You are, perhaps, aware, that the Jewish feast of Pentecost, observed fifty days from the Passover-feast (Lev. xxiii. 15, 16), was the *feast of harvest* (Ex. xxiii. 16), when the first fruits of the wheat harvest were waved before the Lord (Lev. xxiii. 17), the earnest of the harvest soon to be gathered in. In later times, it was also observed, though, so far as we know, without divine authority, in commemoration of the giving of the law. This special day of Pentecost which we are now contemplating is possessed of peculiar significance, in view of these facts; for now the "first fruits" from humanity's white fields are to be offered to God, and the converts of this day are to be but the earnest of the mighty ingathering. Now, also, the *new* law is to be promulgated from Mt. Zion, and the "word of the Lord" is to "go forth from Jerusalem."

Let us, in this letter, mention some of the reasons why this Pentecostal occasion has special significance.

1. *This is the first time that Jesus is heard from, after his ascension.* Condemned on earth by the highest ecclesiastical and civil tribunals known in the land, as worthy of death, he appealed his case to the Supreme Court, and carried up his cause "to Him who judgeth righteously"—to Him who is higher than the highest, before whose dread bar Caiaphas and Pontius Pilate must appear to be judged, and from whose decisions there is no appeal.

On this day we receive tidings, by the divine Spirit-messenger, of the result of the final trial. The unrighteous decisions of the lower courts have been reversed. He who was condemned for blasphemy, because he said, I am the Son of God, is owned in heaven as the Son of God, and all the angels are commanded to worship him. He who was condemned for treason because he said he was a King, is exalted in heaven to the throne of the universe, to reign until all his enemies are subdued. As the authority of Jesus could not be proclaimed until the scandal of these legal decisions was removed, this day furnishes the first opportunity for the inauguration of his reign; for this day he is "justified by the Spirit," and the glorious tidings are announced that "God hath made that same Jesus whom ye have crucified both Lord and Christ."

2. *This is the day the Holy Spirit begins his mission for the conversion of the world.* All through the four Gospels we are reminded of the superior interest attaching to the coming dispensation of the Spirit. John pointed the people away from his baptism to a coming baptism in the Holy Spirit of far greater import. Jesus said to the people, "If any man thirst let him come to me and drink. He that believeth on me, from his inner self shall flow rivers of living water. But this he spoke of the Spirit, which those who believed in him were about to receive; for the Holy Spirit had not yet been given, *because Jesus had not yet been glorified.*" John vii. 37–39. The time has now come, then, when, in the fullest sense of an earthly salvation, the thirsty may come and drink; for Jesus has been glorified, and the Holy Spirit has been given. Please read John, chapters xiv., xv., xvi. You will there learn the importance of the mission of the Spirit, and how impossible it was that the apostles could proceed to open the will of the Lord Jesus, or accomplish any of their ambassadorial functions until the Spirit came to "guide them into all truth."

3. *This day we reach the fulfillment of most important prophecies concerning the dispensation of grace.* Please read carefully Isa. ii. 1–5. Micah iv. 1–3. Psalm cx. All these point forward to the "last days" of the Jewish economy, when a law should go forth from Zion and a word of the Lord from Jerusalem, so powerful, revolutionizing, and regulative as entirely to transform human society. The *time* and the *place of beginning* are both distinctly marked, and are realized on this day of Pentecost.

4. *This day furnishes the first announcement of a complete Gospel of salvation.* All hitherto had been but the *promise* of a salvation yet to be revealed. "The Gospel" is declared by Paul to be, in its essential facts, the death of Christ for our sins, his burial, and resurrection from the dead, for our justification. 1 Cor. xv. 1–4. You will see at a glance that *this* Gospel, "by which we are saved," as Paul affirms, could not be preached as a perfected Gospel until after the resurrection of Jesus. Here, then, we have the *first complete Gospel sermon ever preached in the ears of man. Now*, for the first time can it be said, "all things are ready, come to the wedding."

5. *This day is promulgated the first law ever issued in the name of Jesus Christ.* This may startle you. But it is true. The first law ever issued *in the name*, or by the authority of Jesus Christ, was published on this day, in these words; "Repent and be baptized,

every one of you, IN THE NAME OF JESUS CHRIST, for the remission of sins, and you shall receive the gift of the Holy Spirit." Repentance had been commanded before, but not by the authority of Jesus Christ; baptism had been enjoined before, but not in *this* name; remission of sins had been preached before, but not by this authority. *It is a new law of pardon from a new authority.*

6. *This day Peter, for the first time, uses the "keys of the kingdom of heaven,"* (Matt. xvi. 19), and binds and loosens according to the will of Christ.

Here, therefore, we may learn the terms of entrance into the kingdom of heaven. Why will men puzzle themselves over the enigmatical language of John iii. 1–5, and perpetually appeal, for authority, to a private conversation with Nicodemus, at a time when, for many reasons, Jesus vailed his instructions in parables, when we have here the terms of entrance into the kingdom announced *by authority*, in unfigurative terms, in the literal and positive language of law?

7. *The law of pardon announced this day was to be the law of pardon for all nations and all time.*

"Thus it is written and thus it behooved Christ to suffer, and to rise from the dead the third day: and that *repentance* and *remission of sins* should be preached *in his name*, AMONG ALL NATIONS *beginning* at Jerusalem." Luke xxiv. 46, 47. *Repent* and *be baptized*, every one of you, *in the name of Jesus Christ*, for the *remission of sins.*" Acts ii. 48. Thus they began at Jerusalem to preach, and thus they were to preach to *all nations*, not only for that age, but for all ages; for the promise to them, in fulfilling this commission, is, "Lo, I am with you alway, even unto the end of the world."

Having learned the significance and value of the events of this day of Pentecost, whose history is given to us in the second chapter of Acts, we will, in our next Letter, attempt an analysis of the chapter.

LETTER VII.

Descent of the Holy Spirit—the Audience—the Preacher—the Sermon—its Effects.

We promised to give in this Letter, an analysis of the history of the setting up of the kingdom of Christ, as furnished in the second chapter of Acts. We proceed at once to the task.

I. THE DESCENT OF THE HOLY SPIRIT.

The significance of this fact we have already adverted to. John xiii., xiv. and xv., and John vii. 38, 39, as well as the language of John the Baptist (Matt. iii. 11), point forward to this event as marking an era of superior spiritual blessings. Not that the Holy Spirit had never been given before. But the previous impartations of the Spirit had been limited. This was to be so rich and full and complete a communication of spiritual light and life, that it is called, to denote its abundance, an "*immersion* in the Holy Spirit." And they whose spirits were immersed in these heavenly inspirations, were to be enabled to communicate tidings of salvation and spiritual blessedness such as "eye had not seen, ear had not heard, neither had it entered into the heart of man." 1 Cor. ii. 7–13. Nay, although the Spirit was given "without measure" to Jesus, yet he said concerning the coming ministration of the Spirit: "He that believeth on me, the works that I do shall he do also; and greater works than these shall he do, because I go to my Father." John xiv. 12. We have certainly reached the culmination of the progressive revelations of the divine purposes, when all the treasures of wisdom and knowledge, of grace and mercy, are to be opened. The testator has died—the appointed covenant sacrifice has been offered, and the red seal of the blood of the Lamb of God has been affixed to the will. The executors are assembled, waiting the promised signal of entrance on their duties: "Tarry ye in Jerusalem until ye be endued with power from on high." This power from on high now visits them; their lips are unsealed; their hearts are bathed in the effulgence of heavenly wisdom: they are "filled with the Spirit;" and the tongues of fire that rest on their heads fitly symbolize the searching, burning, purifying energy of the message they are to deliver. The authority of Moses has passed away; the vail of the temple has been rent in twain; and the testimony of the dying Jesus, "It is finished," has closed up the testimony of the law and the prophets, and the authority of them that sat in Moses' seat. The risen Savior has ascended on high, and in the presence of the worshiping angels has been raised to the throne and crowned "Lord of all." The descending Spirit, heralded by a mighty wind, summons those by whom Jesus was condemned, to hear the tidings of the decision of the Supreme Court in the case appealed from them to heaven; and in the very city where Jesus was condemned, and at the next annual festival, when representatives from all parts of the world were there, the load of reproach is to be lifted from his name, that he may be proclaimed as worthy to reign.

II. The Persons on whom the Spirit descended.

We call your attention to the fact that the Spirit was not poured out on *sinners*, but on the *disciples*. The *apostles* were especially enjoined to tarry in Jerusalem until *they* should be endued with power from on high. To *them* accordingly the Spirit came. Jesus said "the world cannot receive" the Spirit. Accordingly, the world does *not* receive it. You, my dear sir, have been waiting these many years for this Spirit to be poured out on you, for your regeneration. Will it not help you out of your difficulty to learn that the Spirit was not promised to sinners—that their regeneration was effected by the Spirit *mediately*, and not by an *immediate* communication? This Spirit was given to *the apostles*, that *through their words* the power symbolized by tongues of fire might reach the hearts of the rebellious. In the largest possible scope of the facts, the Spirit may be said to have been given to the one hundred and twenty disciples who were with the apostles. What then? Why, the Spirit descends on *the Church*—not on *the world;* but reaches the world through the Church. It is easy to be deceived by analogical reasoning. Yet the apostle Paul resorts to it when he says that "no man knoweth the things of a man save the spirit of a man which is in him; even so the things of God knoweth no man, but the Spirit of God." 1 Cor. ii. 11. Without venturing on forbidden ground, we may be allowed to say that this authorized analogy between the spirit of man and the Spirit of God helps us to understand something of the methods through which the Spirit's converting power is put forth. My spirit asserts its power over others *through speech*, communicating my thoughts, reasonings, emotions. So the Spirit of God asserts his convincing and converting power through *words*, addressed by inspired apostles to a sinful world, embodying the thoughts and designs of God in behalf of man, and his reasonings and entreaties with man. But again: my spirit puts forth its power and reveals its life through my body, in my *acts*, so that my whole life and character but reveal the attributes of my spirit. So the Spirit of Christ puts forth life and power through *the Church*—the *body of Christ;* the Church's love, and purity and philanthropy being but a revelation of the life and power of the indwelling Spirit. So that if we contemplate the Spirit as given to the apostles, it is that through the words they speak, the Spirit's power may be communicated to the world; and if we regard the Spirit as given to all the disciples, it is that the mission of the Spirit to convince the world may be accomplished *through the Church.*

We do not pause to speak particularly of the *miraculous* manifestations of the Spirit on this day of Pentecost, farther than to say that what is called the *baptism in the Spirit,* in the only two instances of it on record, is marked by miraculous power; and that therefore this baptism is not to be looked for now. It seems to have been meant more especially to seal Jews and Gentiles with the same Spirit of promise, that they might, by divine certificate, be entitled to equal membership and equal privileges in the kingdom of heaven. See Acts x. 44–47, and xi. 1–18. Thus says Paul, "in one Spirit are we all baptized into one body, whether we be Jews or Gentiles, whether we be bond or free, and have all been made to drink into one Spirit." 1 Cor. xii. 13.

But the most significant fact in these miraculous manifestations is *the gift of tongues*—a clear indication that *by means of language* the converting power of the Holy Spirit was to be put forth. The *immediate* influence of the Spirit was not to convert, but to furnish the recipients with the means of converting others; the *mediate* influence of the Spirit asserted through the gift of tongues, was designed, through the ear, to reach the heart and conscience, that men might "see with their eyes, hear with their ears, understand with their heart, and turn, that their sins might be forgiven them."

III.—The Audience.

These were "Jews, devout men, out of every nation under heaven," who were sojourning at Jerusalem during the annual festivals; as well as many residents of Jerusalem, who had been concerned in the trial and condemnation of Jesus, and who were collected at this time by the rumors of the wonderful phenomena attending the baptism in the Spirit. So far as Christ and his mission were concerned, they were unbelievers; and many of them had been directly or indirectly engaged in procuring his condemnation, or had exulted in his death on the cross. Many thousands were assembled, looking on the tongues of flame, listening to the Gallilean fisherman speaking in various languages which they had never learned, and speculating on the causes of this strange and startling exhibition. Perhaps a more unpromising audience of mockers, bigots, and hard-hearted persecutors never assembled. They were devout, but their very devotion was used to sanctify stubborn unbelief and cruel injustice. They had on their souls the fearful guilt of crucifying the Son of God. Surely if we can see how sinners, such as these, were reconciled to God, we may learn how all others may find mercy.

IV. THE SERMON.

We come now to consider the Sermon of Peter, on the day of Pentecost, and the effects which the Holy Spirit, through the sermon, produced. Please read Acts ii. 14–47.

The discourse opens skillfully. The exordium is an attempt to remove prejudice from the hearers. Many preachers, alas! *create* more prejudice in the rash affirmations of their exordiums, than they are able to dissipate in an hour's subsequent effort. Peter, knowing he must gain their *ears* if he would win their *souls*, carefully removes out of the way the false judgment under which they are laboring. They said " these men are full of new wine." The inspired utterances of the " wonderful works of God," sounded to their prejudiced ears as incoherent babblings. Thus does prejudice or passion pervert the truth of God! It is not enough that we have eyes and ears; we must have a "sound" or "single" eye (Matt. vi. 22), and "circumcised" ears. A superstitious eye transformed the loving Savior into a frightful specter (Matt. xiv. 26); the approving voice of the Father was, to unbelieving ears, but thunder (John xii. 29); while to the honest, cultivated ear of Mary, the voice of the Master was the end of darkness—the gay dawn of immortal blessedness. (John xx. 16.) These are facts of grave import. Well did Jesus say, "Take heed *how* ye hear." Peter, therefore, proceeds first to dispossess his hearers of prejudice, by unfolding the phenomena on which they gazed as the fulfillment of one of the grand predictions of their own Scriptures: a fulfillment which would usher in the period they were all so anxiously looking for, as "the last days"—the days of the Messiah. "This is that which was spoken of by the prophet Joel: It shall come to pass in the last days, saith God, that I will pour out of my Spirit on all flesh; and your sons and your daughters shall prophesy; and your young men shall see visions, and your old men shall dream dreams. And also on my servants and on my handmaids I will pour out my Spirit in those days, and they shall prophesy. And I will show wonders in heaven above, and signs in the earth beneath, blood and fire and columns of smoke. The sun shall be turned into darkness and the moon into blood before that great and terrible day of the Lord comes. And it shall come to pass that whoever shall call on the name of the Lord shall be saved."

This introduction must not be passed over carelessly. If the occasion possesses the significance we have given to it, this opening sermon of the kingdom is pregnant with meaning. We have only space to hint at some of its suggestive utterances; and, in the light of our preceding discussions, we have hopes that hints will now suffice.

1. The phrase "last days," marks the culminating point in the history of redemption. Up to this time, the word of God had authorised men to look forward to better things to come. The "last days" had not yet been reached. But now we enter on the period of "the *last* days." This is the *first* of the "last days." We suppose the phrase rightfully includes the whole period of Messiah's reign. There are no *other* days to follow—no future changes to be anticipated in the unfoldings of the plan of redemption. The "fullness of time" has been reached; and a perfect, permanent, unchangeable covenant and priesthood are now established; and a "kingdom that cannot be moved" is received. Here is "Inquirer's" resting-place.

2. This outpouring of the Spirit marks an era of *philanthropy* such as had never been witnessed or dreamed of. In a representa-

tive sense it is the baptism of *humanity* in the Spirit of God; for all classes, ranks, ages, and nationalities are embraced in it. Jew—Gentile, "all flesh;" old—young; men—women; masters—slaves; thus marking all ranks, conditions, and races, as equally entitled to share in the blessings of the kingdom of heaven. All are made to drink into one Spirit. Evidently we have passed away from the religion of the Family, which marked the patriarchal age; and the religion of the Nation, which marked the Mosaical dispensation, into the fullest development of the "unsearchable riches of Christ,"—the riches of wisdom, mercy and life for *man* as man—for "all the world." If, any where, you are to find the mercy of God intended for *you*, it will certainly be found here.

3. The language, in its bold symbols, marks *revolution* as a necessary result of proclaiming the kingdom of God. It is foreign to our purpose to search for the precise meaning and application of the language of verses 19, 20. Suffice it to say that it clearly indicates the overthrow of political or ecclesiastical establishments, or both; as Paul says (Heb. xii. 29), "the removing of the things that are shaken, as of things that are made, that the things that cannot be shaken may remain. Wherefore, as we receive a kingdom which cannot be shaken, let us have grace, whereby we may serve God acceptably, with reverence and godly fear; for

our God is a consuming fire." All that was preparatory, adumbrative, and ancillary, as well as all that was antagonistical, must now give way to the kingdom of heaven, which was promised to "break in pieces and consume" all other kingdoms.

The *theme* of this sermon is JESUS. It is not a sermon on the law, on regeneration, election, effectual calling, freedom of the will, or any of the thousand and one topics of theological warfare, the discussion of which has so bewildered your mind. Jesus promised the apostles, that when the Spirit of truth came, "he shall take of mine and shall show it unto you;" "he shall testify concerning me." John xv. 26, and xvi. 14. Accordingly the Spirit's testimony, as delivered by Peter, is all concerning Jesus. "I determined not to know any thing among you, but Jesus Christ and him crucified," said Paul. A return to the integrity of the primitive Gospel would, my dear sir, be an end to all your troubles. Instead of troubling yourself with psychological phenomena to ascertain whether you are regenerated, or with knotty theologies to ascertain whether you are numbered with the elect, or with the legalisms of an economy that has passed away, you should first settle the question, Whether this Jesus whom the apostles preached, is the promised Christ? and then, secondly, inquire, Do I so trust in and love Him as to be willing to renounce all other sovereignties and obey only Him? The point reached of intelligent trust in Him as the Son of God, and entire submission to Him of heart and life, as the rightful Lord and Savior, all important questions touching our salvation are settled—for the promises are made to such as *believe* and *obey.*

Accordingly, Jesus, in his wonderful works, Jesus in his death on the cross, Jesus in his resurrection from the dead, Jesus in his exaltation and glorification, Jesus in his kingly power and authority, is the theme of this discourse. The strength of the discourse is expended on his resurrection and exaltation, because the facts previously stated were indisputable, and because the Christhood of Jesus depended on his resurrection. If he had not been raised from the dead, then his cause had failed of divine vindication, and they who had condemned him were justified. But if he had been raised from the dead, God had vindicated his cause, and his enemies were loaded with fearful guilt in condemning and crucifying their own Messiah. This grand fact is proved, therefore, 1. By their own Scriptures, by passages which they admitted to refer to the promised Messiah. 2. By the testimony of eye-witnesses: "whereof we all are witnesses." 3. By the supernatural manifestations of that occasion. "Wherefore being by the right hand of God exalted, and having received the promise of the Holy Spirit, he has shed forth this which you see and hear." Thus, step by step, he approaches an irresistible conclusion—a conclusion armed with unspeakable terrors to his guilty auditors: "*Let all the house of Israel know assuredly that God hath made that same Jesus whom you crucified both Lord and Christ.*"

The narrative states that "when they heard this, they were pierced to the heart, and said to Peter and the rest of the apostles, what shall we do?" The language indicates the most pungent conviction and harrowing distress of mind. Here, then, was something that reached stubborn and rebellious hearts, and broke them to pieces as the hammer breaks the rock. What was it? Not the outpouring of the Spirit, for we have seen that the Spirit was not poured out on the ungodly. What then? "*When they heard this*, they were pierced to the heart." It was *the truth that Peter proclaimed*, and the evidences which Peter arrayed, establishing conviction in their hearts of the Christhood and Lordship of the risen Jesus. The Spirit's converting power was put forth then, through Peter's sermon, and this converting power went in *through their ears* into the understanding, and by this route reached the conscience and the heart. Did it ever strike you, Mr. Inquirer, while you were waiting for regenerating power to visit your heart, that the power of God comes in *through the ears?* and that the truth which the Spirit has set forth for your salvation is waiting an entrance through this ordained channel into your soul? "*Incline your ear* and come unto me; *hear*, and your soul shall live." "Say not in thy heart, who shall ascend into heaven; that is to bring down Christ from above; or, who shall descend into the abyss; that is to bring Christ again from the dead. But what saith it? *The word is nigh thee*, in thy mouth and in thy heart: that is, *the word of faith which we preach:* that if thou wilt confess with the mouth the Lord Jesus, and believe in thy heart that God has raised him from the dead, thou shalt be saved." Rom. x. 6–9.

The powerful convictions produced by this discourse, brought on a crisis in the day's affairs. Thousands of anguished sinners confess their guilt, and throw themselves at the feet of the King's ambassadors, and sue for mercy. The first acts of a monarch's reign are taken as indicative of the character and spirit of his government. The beginning of the legal dispensation was marked by the execution of about three thousand offenders. (Ex. xxxii. 25–28.) Thus did the stern spirit of Law frown darkly on the guilty, and foreshadow "the ministration of death, written and engraven in stones." Here are about an equal number of offenders to be disposed of, at the beginning of the reign of Jesus. What will he do with them? They are his own murderers, stained with the guilt of a crime that has no adequate name—which, for the want of a better term, we call *deicide*.

What will he do with these men that spit on him, and cried, "not this man, but Barabbas," and gave him up to Roman hands to be scourged, and mocked, and crucified? The disposition made of this case will indicate the character of the newly exalted King, and the genius and spirit of his reign. And what a blessed revelation it proves to be! The law commenced with three thousand slain under the law's condemnation; the Gospel commences with three thousand made alive, pardoned and justified by the grace of God! Listen, ye guilty and perishing! The man with the keys of the Kingdom of Heaven on his shoulder, is about to open the gates of salvation; the executors are about to open the will of the Lord Jesus; the ambassadors are in a moment to proclaim the authority of the new King in Zion. The fate of thousands present and millions absent, hangs on his words. Will they be words of mercy and peace, or of wrath and vengeance? Our hopes for time and eternity are resting on the clemency and mercy of the King. Listen! "Repent and be baptized, every one of you, in the name of Jesus Christ, for the remission of sins, and you shall receive the gift of the Holy Spirit."

Glory to God! The reign of heaven is a reign of *mercy! Jerusalem* sinners are saved! The first act of the King is to pardon his suppliant enemies—his murderers! The first names written on the rolls of the ransomed, since his assumption of royalty, are taken from among those who rejected him and mocked his dying pangs! Then there is mercy for *all* the broken-hearted and despairing of earth's guilty children.

It will require another Letter to complete our examination of this narrative. We are proceeding leisurely, because a proper understanding of this chapter is an end to doubt and confusion on the subject of your inquiries.

LETTER VIII.

What must we do to be Saved?—A new Institution.

We propose, in this Letter, to complete our examination of the second chapter of Acts.

The question propounded by the convicted hearers was, *What shall we do?* A singular question in the light of modern theology! That on which the greatest stress is now laid, is the doctrine of utter passivity in regeneration. Man is utterly helpless, can do nothing, ought to do nothing,—never can be saved until he consents to do nothing! One of the most popular of modern revival hymns, has lines something like these:

> "Doing is a deadly thing—
> Cast down all your doing."

The creed in which you have been educated asserts that man is "wholly passive" in regeneration. In Fisher's Catechism, faith is represented to be "a work that requires almighty power, even the same power that was wrought in Christ, when he was raised from the dead. Eph. i. 19, 20." Page 140, part I.

> "Ques. 43. Why cannot man co-operate with God in this work (regeneration)?"
>
> "Ans. Because there can be no acting without a principle of action. Regeneration being the infusing of spiritual life into the soul, it is impossible the creature can co-operate or concur with God in it, *any more than Lazarus in the grave could concur in his own resurrection*, till the powerful voice of Christ infused life and strength into him." P. 144, part II.

This is, indeed, to be "wholly passive." And you have doubtless long since reflected that if this is a fair representation of your spiritual condition, you are no more to be blamed for your failure to be a Christian, than a dead man can be blamed for not rising from the dead! Regeneration is a question of naked omnipotence. In that case, surely, there is nothing to "do." But these sinners asked, in their anguish, "What shall we *do?*" And the answer did not relieve them from the conviction that something must be *done*. Now, if, when it is said, "doing is a deadly thing," it means trusting to what we do as a meritorious cause of salvation, we can cordially approve it; but when this doctrine of utter passivity is broached, we not only demur, but we denounce it as one of the most deadly errors to which the soul of man can be enslaved. For it robs man of the privilege and duty of saving himself, according to Peter's exhortation—"Save yourselves from this untoward generation;" and relieves him of all responsibility for his rejection of the Gospel—at the same time consigning him to eternal condemnation for failing to do that which, in his utter deadness, he could not possibly do. It is absurd as well. Why dehort a *dead* man *against* doing? How absurd to attempt to thunder into the ears of those who are locked in the sleep of the grave,

"Doing is a deadly thing!"

The apostle not only did not teach these sinners that there was nothing to be done, but he *did* teach them that they *must* do certain things, if they would be saved. "Repent and be baptized, every one of you, in the name of Jesus Christ, for remission of sins," etc.

It will not meet this difficulty to say that these sinners were regenerated by a miracle before they cried out, "What shall we do?" For, (1.) The theology with which we are dealing, teaches that there is no difference in point of time between faith and repentance; and on that principle, as repentance was enjoined on those sinners as a duty not yet accomplished, it is clear that faith had not yet been wrought in their hearts; and, (2.) As we cannot conceive of a regenerated person still unpardoned and unblessed with the Holy Spirit, these persons were evidently unregenerated, since they had not yet received the remission of sins nor the gift of the Holy Spirit. Rely on it, therefore, something must be *done*, on *your* part, before you are saved. God has done much to save us—without which we could do nothing. But now that God has completed his part in the work of redemption, it remains that we do, on our part, what is necessary to make his salvation ours. And what must the sinner do?

One thing these sinners had already done: *they had accepted Peter's preaching as true*—they had *believed* his testimony concerning the Christ. They had now laid on them two additional commandments. 1. Repent. 2. Be baptized, in the name of Jesus Christ. We shall not pause to consider the meaning of these precepts. That will occupy future letters. We will only refer to it so far as to say that in that which they had done, and that which they were farther told to do, there is involved a threefold change—a change which embraces in it all that we call regeneration and conversion. It stands thus:

1. Faith—resulting in a *change of heart*, or a purification of affections.

2. Repentance—or *a change of conduct*—a "turning from sin to Christ, with a sincere

purpose and endeavor to walk with him in all the ways of his commandments."

3. BAPTISM—or *a change of state;* a translation out of the world into the kingdom of God's beloved Son; out of a state of condemnation into a state of justification.

This threefold change brings us into the full blessings of citizenship in the kingdom of heaven; so that, to all the subjects of it, the language of the apostle may be rightfully applied: "So then you are no more strangers and foreigners, but fellow-citizens with the saints, and of the household of God." Eph. ii. 19. And to all who thus enter the kingdom, its threefold treasures of grace rightfully belong; "righteousness, peace, and joy in the Holy Spirit." Rom. xvi. 17. Pardon, adoption, and heirship are theirs, by covenant promise and seal, according to the will and testament of our Lord and Savior Jesus Christ.

In the light of these facts we reach several conclusions which we will now state.

1. *The Jewish and Christian institutions are not the same.* All these converts to Christ were Jews—lawful members of that institution. But this did not entitle them to membership in the Christian institution. They were "added to the church" of Christ by virtue of a new birth—a regeneration by water and Spirit; or, in plain terms, by their faith in Christ, their repentance toward God, and their baptism in the name of the Lord

Jesus. The term *Church*, used Acts ii. 47 (ekkleesia), is an assembly called out, summoned forth, separated, insulated for a special purpose. These converts were called out and separated *from the Jewish institution*, for purposes which that institution could not accomplish. The "church" is a new affair, very different from the *nation*. It has a new king, a new lawgiver, a new covenant, new conditions of membership, new laws and ordinances, new aims and a new spirit: "old things are passed away, behold all things are become new." The new wine is put into new bottles. The institutions have a point of connection, because one was a type of the other, one prepared the way for the other—but in that sense only.

2. *Baptism did not come in the room of circumcision.* These converts were all in "the covenant of circumcision," yet they were all baptized. How absurd, then, to say that one came in room of the other!

3. *Infant membership is not recognized in this kingdom.* "They that gladly received the word were baptized." Verse 41. They can be members only by *voluntary acceptance* of its terms. True, it says "the promise is to you, and to your children, and to all that are afar off, even as many as the Lord, our God, shall call." But, 1. Baptism is not a *promise*, but a *commandment*. 2. Children being mentioned, does not prove that they are members of the church any more than "all that are afar off"

proves that they were members. They could all be such by obeying the *call:* "even as many as the Lord our God shall call."

4. *The facts of this chapter furnish the safest interpretation of John iii.* 5. The birth of water and Spirit was entrance into the kingdom of God. Now here about three thousand enter the kingdom. The man with the keys of "the kingdom of heaven" is here, and opens the gate of salvation. What do we find? 1. The Spirit, by means of the preaching of the apostles, bringing sinners to believe and repent;—convicting them of sin, of righteousness, and of judgment. 2. Those who are thus brought to repentance are baptized and added to the church. Thus they were "born of water and of the Spirit." Why be perplexed with the language of a passage almost enigmatical, when these plain facts unfold, in perfect simplicity, the mode of entrance into the kingdom? The Spirit is here; the water is here; and here are the sinners who, by means of these agencies, are made new creatures in Christ Jesus. The truth is translated out of the realm of parable into the realm of fact, and, in the translation, loses all mysteriousness.

It would be interesting to note the *results* of the conversion of these thousands, as detailed in the latter part of the chapter; but that would take us beyond the "first principles" to which these letters are confined. We will only note that they "continued steadfastly in the apostles' teaching"—not in the law of Moses; a fact clearly indicative of a new order of things.

5. Finally, we observe that the kingdom which you see in this chapter as a "little stone" cut out "without hands," and propelled by divine power, is to "become a great mountain and fill the whole earth." The "repentance and remission of sins" here preached, are to be preached to "all nations." The will here opened is the *last* will and testament. The sun has risen. The stars cease to shine. The light of no brighter sun will be kindled. The salvation of God in its fullness is revealed. "It is finished." The feast is spread. The oxen and fatlings are killed, and "all things are ready." "The Spirit and the Bride say, Come. And let him that heareth it say, Come. Let him who is athirst, come. And whosoever will, let him drink of the water freely."

Letter from an Inquirer.—II.

To the Editor of the Christian Standard:

I have refrained from expressing my thanks for your very courteous treatment of my former letter, because I did not desire to interrupt your connected reasonings. I have followed you with lively interest through your series of letters, and cannot longer refrain from telling you how greatly I am indebted to you for your clear, and to me very novel, style of disposing of my perplexities. I have been much surprised at some of your avowals. I had been led to believe that you were advocating a new-fangled religion; and, to be candid with you, I half wished it would prove so—so weary was I of attempting to make sense out of the theology in which I had been educated, that I had at least half a desire to be persuaded into Broad Church Liberalism; and wrote to you in hope that you would lead me out in that direction. But I am disappointed. While you are, indeed, liberal, in casting off the bondage of human authority; and while I cheerfully acknowledge much relief in the view you present of the Old Testament and its authority, I cannot but regard you as among the most rigid advocates of the authority of the New Testament. Will you allow me to say that I fear your rigid adherence to the letter of the New Testament will not suit these times? I almost think that the mere forms of religion, such as baptism, and verbal prayer, and Sabbath observances; and such doctrines as the divinity of Christ, and the atonement, belong to the dead past; and that in this stage of the world's progress we may be allowed to cast off the swaddling-bands of infancy, and attain to a freer development of soul. You ask me if I do not love Jesus? I answer, yes; I love *his character*. I greatly admire and love his goodness, and purity, and benevolence; and if I follow him in these, why should I be burdened with doctrines, and forms, and the conventional restraints of church associations? Now, please do not condemn me as an infidel. I am not. These are thoughts—dreams—that sometimes take possession of me, imbibed, perhaps, from my more recent readings. And when I shake these off, I find myself gliding back into my early convictions. And so, while at one time, you seem to be not half liberal enough, at another you appear to have gone too far; and I fear that, in denying the authority of Moses, you have broken the tables of the law over again, and left us without an inspired code of morals. Now, can you bear with me in these strange contradictions? Do you know any way to help me out of these jungles? I have, since writing to you, heard some of your preachers; but I cannot say that they did me much good. They seem to me to be enslaved to the mere letter of Scripture, without regard to its spirit, and the most of their preaching is to establish an intellectual faith, and to persuade people to "make confession" and be immersed. I am glad to learn, incidentally from your letters, that baptism is not regarded by you as a panacea for all spiritual ailments—a plaster to cover all the wounds of sin; and that faith is something more than a mere assent to the truth. Yet I have listened to your preachers, when no one could be blamed for receiving these impressions; yet, perhaps, it was my own unhappy mind, rather than any fault of theirs, that gave such a tinge to the preaching.

I am anxious to hear you still farther. I do not present objections in a formal way, but prefer to state in a general way my state of mind, and leave you to dispose of it as you go along, without interfering with the plan of your letters. I wish your readers to believe me when I say that I would not be guilty of the egotism of thrusting myself and my spiritual troubles upon the public, did I not know that I am unfortunately a representative of a large class, especially of the young men of this time. They cannot wed their souls to the doctrines of a past age. Yet they want to be religious. They are rapidly drifting into Broad Church views and sympathies. It will be a blessing to many if you can lead them out of their bewilderments.

AN INQUIRER.

LETTER IX.

Extremes of Roman Catholicism and Rationalism—Unbelief the root of both, as well as of Sectarianism—The Godship of Jesus—Folly of the pretense of believing in Him while rejecting his authority.

You are *beginning* to discern our true position. It is true that, on one hand, we renounce and oppose all ***human*** authority in religion—not only as claimed and urged by the Roman Catholic advocates of church authority, but as it is embodied in the creed authority, systems of divinity, and man-ordained rites of the Protestant Evangelicals. The present controversy on Ritualism is only beginning to unmask the "commandments and traditions of men," which Protestants have foisted into their theology and their worship. Before it is over, even the anti-ritualists will have found that they, too, have some of "the accursed thing" hidden in *their* tents; and many a Babylonish garment, and wedge of gold, and shekel of silver, will have to be given to destruction in the valley of Achor ere the hosts of Israel can march on to certain victory. Josh. vii.

It is equally true, on the other hand, that we are as sternly opposed to the human authority which the false Liberalism of this time asserts. This is, in fact, but a new shoot from the same root. *Unbelief* is the root of all these mischiefs, whether in the form of absolute submission to human authority, as in the Roman Catholic Church; or in adulteration of divine teaching with creed authority, as among Protestants; or in the rejection of Scripture authority and the deification of Reason, as among the Liberalists and Rationalists. Against them all we lift up the standard of the LORDSHIP OF JESUS, and insist on absolute submission to a Divine Savior, and to him *alone*. In this you understand us correctly.

It is not surprising that, in seeking to escape from the embarrassments and confusions of your early religious convictions, you should be exposed to the dangers of another and more perilous extreme. This is the operation of a law of mind as certain and inevitable in its workings as any law in the universe of mind. It is subject, however, to modifications by the presence and power of other equally potent laws; and our hope, in your case, is that, before you sweep too far past the center, in your escape from the bondage of a speculative theology, you will be arrested by the simplicity and consistency of New Testament teachings, and that your soul will be fastened by the sweet and pure attractions of that Son of Mary and Son of God, whose human excellence you so readily admit — whose divine attractions and claims you will find it difficult to deny, without violently wrenching judgment, faith, and conscience, all. If you have been confused and oppressed by the unreasonable and contradictory teachings of the old Calvinistic theology, do not think you will find rest by escaping into the endless labyrinths of modern Rationalism. There is no *rock* in that region of quicksands, on which your weary soul can rest. It is a region of mists and fogs, of desert and mirage and phantasm. No unlettered boor ever followed a jack-with-the-lantern through deeper mire, with more eager credulity, to a more hopeless terminus, than do these enlightened rationalists, in their earnest pursuit of scientific religion. One thing is certain: since Jesus of Nazareth, no other has arisen who can dispute with him the palm. Eighteen hundred years of experiment and progress have not improved on his character and teachings. No other Christ has arisen who could challenge the love and adoration of the human heart: no Sufferer, no Toiler, no Teacher, no Philanthropist, no Leader and Sovereign like Him. He is "the lone miracle of History," even to the infidel world. We gain nothing, but lose everything, in losing Him. If He is true, we gain all by clinging to him; if He is false, we still gain nothing by forsaking Him. There is left to us no Guide, no Savior. We are thrown back on ourselves—the very self we sought to be delivered from—to walk in the light of our own reason, conscience, intuitions; and then, every man's conscience, reason, intuitions, *are just what he wants them to be:* interest, passion, associations, or former habitudes, subjecting them to impressment, and compelling them to give forth oracles to suit the ruling passion of the hour. Is there "rest for the weary" in *that* direction? Pause, and consider well, I pray you, ere you turn your back on the Sun of Righteousness, to be led —not even by a fixed star in the heavens, but by an *ignis fatuus* springing from the decompositions of the morasses and grave-yards of the dead Past.

You think us rigid in insisting on absolute submission to Jesus the Christ. That, no doubt, is the very battle-ground where, if you ever surrender to Christ, your last battle will be fought. You think we are enslaved to the *letter* of the New Testament. Perhaps, in some cases, this may be true, without a consciousness of it on our part. We do not know how to reach the spirit of any Scripture except through the letter; but we care not for the mere letter except as helping us to the *meaning* of the speaker or writer. We do not desire to be content with the hull and fail to reach the kernel. We care not to get *words*, and fail to obtain the meaning. But you shall judge whether it is letter, or spirit, or both, when we tell you that no confession of faith, no totality of immersion, weigh so much as a feather with us *unaccompanied with the absolute surrender of life and destiny—judgment, conscience, heart, and character, to the control and disposal of the Lord Jesus Christ.* Is not that *spiritual* and *evangelical* enough for you, even in your most orthodox moods? Nothing else will satisfy the demands of the letter *and* spirit of the New Testament.

You say you "admire and love the *character* of Jesus," etc. Did you reflect, in saying this, that unless he is really divine, and did really die for our sins, and rise for our justification, he has no character that an honest heart can respect? He claimed to be the Son of God—to have life in himself—to be the only way to truth and life—to die for the sins of the world—to rise from the grave to Lordship and Christhood, to be the Savior and the king of men. Based on these claims of divinity and authority, he sent forth his apostles, commanding them to disciple the nations, baptizing them into the name of the Father and of the Son and of the Holy Spirit. Now, was he *deceived in himself*, in making these claims, thus evincing himself to be an amiable enthusiast merely? or did he *deceive others*—thus proving himself to be guilty of falsehood and fraud to serve his own ambitions? In either case how can you admire his *character*, and desire to imitate *that* as the sum of all religion? No, sir: if Jesus has a *character* worthy of your admiration, it is because *he was what he professed to be.* And in that case, you must accept his divinity, his atonement, and his ordinances too.

We have not room to notice at present all

the points in your letter. They will not be forgotten. Neither must you forget that we are writing for thousands beside yourself; and that, while these letters are addressed to you, they must necessarily embrace the wants and the difficulties of many who are not in your position. We hope to meet a variety of wants before we close. Meanwhile we shall be pleased to receive your suggestions, and not less pleased because they express frank dissent from our own convictions. "Prove all things; hold fast that which is good."

LETTER X.

The sinner required to save himself.

Having led you through the Old Testament, and the four Gospels, to the culminating point in the history of redemption; and having learned the authority under which we are placed—even that of the Lord Jesus; and the ambassadors who are authorized to speak in his name—even the twelve apostles; we feel, just at this point, like preaching you a little sermon from a text to be found in this second chapter of Acts, verse fortieth:

"*Save yourselves from this untoward generation.*"

You see that, after all, men are required to *save themselves.* It is simply impossible that man can be entirely passive in coming into possession of this salvation. It is a salvation from *sin*. Can man be saved from sin without *renouncing* it? Can he renounce it, until he ceases to *love* it? Can he cease to love it, until he takes into his understanding the stern and terrible truths which exhibit its odiousness and deformity? Moreover, to be saved by the Lord Jesus he must *trust* him and *love* him. Can he trust and love without an *exercise* of his thoughts and affections? Still farther: the enjoyment of this salvation is suspended on *obedience*. The sinner is required to "repent and be baptized." Now, this obedience necessitates the activity alike of the intellectual, moral, and physical powers, in thinking, purposing, and acting. There can be nothing worthy the name of salvation to an intelligent nature, which does not involve an active participation in the process on the part of the nature that is saved. Insensate matter may be entirely passive in undergoing change; but a thinking, willing, responsible spirit, never. However absolute, therefore, some passages may seem to represent the work of God in saving men to be, it must be always understood, whether expressed or not, that its success is contingent on the acquiescence of the rational nature which is addressed.

Let us furnish an illustration of this point: In Acts xxvii., we have an account of a fearful peril on shipboard—a peril so great that passengers and crew were abandoned to utter despair. Paul assured them all, however, on the ground of a special revelation from an angel of God, that there should be no loss of any man's life among them. The revelation was: "Lo, God hath given thee all them that sail with thee." Verse 24. This seems as absolute and unconditional as language can make it. It looks as if they had simply *to be saved.* Yet (verse 31), when the sailors were about to abandon the vessel, Paul said to the centurion, "Except these abide in the ship, *ye cannot be saved.*" And when, finally, the ship was guided to a suitable place and run aground, and the hinder part of the vessel was broken in pieces—they were not lifted on angels' wings to the shore, but—such as could swim, *swam* to land; "and the rest, some on boards, and some on broken pieces of the ship. And *so* it came to pass that they escaped all safe to land." Verses 43, 44. Now, was this a divine salvation? Certainly. The unseen hand of God—the power that rides on the whirlwind and directs the storm—guided this frail vessel through the perils of the deep to a suitable retreat; and had it not been for this divine guidance they must have perished. But, as soon as their salvation was made attainable—as soon as it was brought within reach of their own powers, they were required to *save themselves;* in other words, they were called on *to appropriate* the deliverance which God had opened, each to himself, by the exercise of his own powers. Had they not done so, they would not have been saved.

So, in the salvation of the soul from sin, God does for us what we cannot do for ourselves. We could not by searching find out God. God reveals himself in Jesus Christ that we may know him. We cannot create the truths or the inspirations by which the soul is to be lifted out of the mire of ignorance and pollution. God has, by his Spirit, brought these to us. We cannot ransom our souls from guilt, or atone for the sins we have committed. God has given his own Son to be a Ransom for us, and to become righteousness to the believer. We cannot discover a pathway to heaven, or uncover the awful mysteries of eternity. God has, by the resurrection of Jesus, scattered the darkness of death, and brought life to light. We cannot believe, or repent, or turn to good, except as our thoughts and affections are receptive of divine influences. God pours these divine influences upon us through the Gospel revelations. So evident is it that salvation is of the Lord, and that, if saved at all, we are saved by the grace of God.

Yet the text says, "*Save yourselves.*" Yes: because, notwithstanding all that has been done to save us, we are still unsaved until we accept and appropriate the salvation of

God, by complying with the conditions of the Gospel. The sun shines in vain, unless we open our eyes to behold it, that we may walk in its light; so truth is revealed in vain, and Jesus lives and loves and dies and rises in vain, unless we look and believe. Bread for the starving is furnished in vain, unless they take and eat it; so the Gospel feast is spread in vain, unless we "*come* to the wedding," and eat of the bread of life, and drink of the waters of salvation.

But you ask, is not man contemplated in the Gospel as helpless—dead? Yes. But not in the absolute sense that is often attached to the words. There are different degrees of helplessness. A dead body floating on a stream, or lying in the bed of a river, is *entirely* passive; and if brought out at all, must be brought out *by main force.* But a man may be likely to drown, in the river, who is not so utterly helpless. Left to himself he will perish; but if a hand is stretched forth to save him, he can grasp it, and thus both save himself and be saved. Sinners left to themselves will perish. But they have eyes, ears, minds, hearts; and can see, hear, reason, feel, and act, when the salvation of God is brought within their reach. The sinner is, indeed, said to be dead—dead in sins; that is, his sins have separated him from the friendship and fellowship of God. But a man can be dead in one sense and alive in another. He may be spiritually dead, yet intellectually as well as physically alive. He has mind, heart, and conscience, to which God can appeal, and through which he may be reached with truth and love for his salvation. Hence this exhortation—"Save yourselves"—does not come until all the divine potencies for our salvation have first been brought to bear.

We have, then, in this sermon of Peter on the day of Pentecost,

I. FACTS—revealing what God *has done* for our salvation. These facts embrace the incarnation, life, death, and resurrection of the Son of God.

II. COMMANDMENTS—revealing what *we must do* to be saved. These are,

1. Believe on the Lord Jesus Christ.
2. Repent.
3. Be baptized, in the name of Jesus Christ.

III. PROMISES—revealing what God *will do* for those who obey the Gospel. These are,

1. Remission of sins.
2. The gift of the Holy Spirit.
3. Citizenship in the kingdom—heirship in the family of God.

Thus, facts to be *believed*, commandments to be *obeyed*, and promises to be *enjoyed*, make up this Gospel, and embrace both the divine and human sides of this scheme of salvation.

We are now prepared to speak more definitely of the things that *we* must do to be saved. On this we will enter in our next number.

Meanwhile, let us ask you to reflect on another distinction which, sooner or later, you will need to be made acquainted with.

While we have insisted on the importance of man's consenting to save himself by closing in with the overtures of mercy, it is evident that all he is asked to do is *to accept* the salvation. Faith, repentance, and baptism are but graciously ordained means of *appropriating* the grace of God; so that it is, after all, a salvation "not of works," but of grace. There is *another* salvation, however, with which active obedience is more emphatically linked—so much so that we are enjoined to "work out our salvation." The first salvation tendered in the Gospel is salvation from the guilt and dominion of sin, and is enjoyed on our simple submission to Christ, before we begin active work in his service. But there is a coming salvation *from death*—an entrance into life eternal, which is made to rest—not on faith merely, but—on character. "Be thou faithful unto death, and I will give thee a crown of life." "Blessed are they that do his commandments, that they may have right to the tree of life, and enter in through the gates into the city." This salvation lies rather out of the range of our present inquiries; so we merely note it here for the sake of avoiding confusion of mind.

6

LETTER XI.

Faith—Its Meaning—Not the product of Almightiness—Not mere assent to Truth—Has a moral element in its Scriptural meaning—Reliance on a thing or person as true and worthy—Its sources, value, and adaptedness to our nature.

We come now to consider *the terms of salvation*, or, what we must do to make this salvation ours. We have already seen that there are three conditions—Faith, Repentance, and Baptism. We devote this letter to a consideration of FAITH. This is the first in order, as we learn from the answer given to an inquirer who had as yet taken no step toward Christ—whose question was extorted by the alarm of an earthquake, and not by any knowledge of this salvation. Acts xvi. 30, 31. "Sirs, what must I do to be saved?" was the anxious inquiry. The answer was: "Believe on the Lord Jesus Christ, and thou shalt be saved, and thy house."

We have already hinted that these conditions are not arbitrary—that they are wisely and graciously adapted to the capacities and wants of our nature. It is essential to a proper appreciation of the Gospel that this be understood, for we are persuaded that the repulsiveness of these conditions to many minds grows out of the legalistic and ritualistic aspects in which they are taught to view them. When they come to see that these terms are not mere arbitrary forms, nor assertions of dogmatic authority, but wise and merciful adaptations to the capacities and predicaments of our nature, these conditions of salvation will become as attractive to them as they were before repulsive.

But before we can learn the adaptations of Faith to our nature and circumstances, we must understand what Faith is. It is unquestionably true, as Pollock says, that "Faith was bewildered much by men who meant to make it clear." This grows largely out of the efforts at logical consistency in the construction of theological systems. Men form theories of the divine nature and of human nature, and then torture every item of Scripture teaching that seems to bear against them, into submission. When the doctrine of *total depravity* is once accepted, regeneration must needs be a miracle, and faith the immediate product of almightiness. No one thing has done more to make the Gospel unlovely to men, than, first, to make the terms of salvation binding on the sinner; and, secondly, teach the impossibility of his performing them.

We remember to have heard a clergyman (he is yet living) acknowledge that he had for many years taught that faith was *a spiritual substance* which dropped from the hand of God into the sinner's heart. His proof text was Heb. xi, 1. "Now faith is the *substance* of things hoped for." Here, he triumphantly affirmed, it is declared to be a *substance*—a substance to be "hoped for" until the sinner gets it! He did not know that the Latin *substantia* was from *substans*, pres. part. of *substare*, to stand under; nor that the Greek *hupostasis*, in its original meaning, is *that whereon anything else stands, or is supported;* that faith is, therefore, that which *stands under* the things hoped for—the foundation, indeed, of Christian life, hope, consolation, and victory.

Your old theological standards, my dear sir, are not at all more sensible in their teachings concerning faith.

"*Ques.* 11. Why can no less a worker than the Spirit of God work this faith?

Ans. Because it is a work that requires *almighty power*, even the same power which was wrought in Jesus when he was raised from the dead. Eph. i. 19, 20." Fisher's Catechism, p. 139.

There is as much good sense in asserting that the power which propels a railroad train is the very same power that demonstrates mathematical problems, as in this affirmation that the omnipotence which raised Jesus from the dead is the power that produces faith. It is an absurdity into which good men could never have been led, had they not first been possessed of the conviction of the utter depravity of human nature,—so that, there being no starting place within a mass of utter corruption, regeneration must needs begin in miracle. As well talk of digging into a man's soul with a spade, to prepare it, by physical culture, to become the garden of the Lord. *Mind must be reached in harmony with the laws of mind.*

Is it any wonder that men object to being condemned for unbelief, when there is no escape from it except by miracle?

"Faith is the belief of testimony," says another, "and no man is, therefore, responsible for his belief. If the testimony is sufficient, he is compelled to believé, whether he wants to or not. If the testimony is insufficient, he cannot believe, no matter how much he desires to do so. Faith is *involuntary.* It is, therefore, arbitrary and unjust, to suspend salvation on that over which we have no control."

These are but a few of the various crudities concerning faith with which the religious world abounds. They will serve to teach us the importance of clear, definite, and Scriptural ideas, unencumbered with the endless confusions of philosophers and theologians.

We ask, then, what is the meaning of the word *faith?*

1. The classical sense of *pistis* is, trust in others, especially faith or belief in a higher power; persuasion of a thing, confidence, assurance. Subjectively, it means, good faith, faithfulness, honesty.

2. The current use of the word does not differ materially from this. Its usual mean-

ing is, confiding in a thing or person as true and worthy. Hence we say of men, "I have faith in that general;" or, "I have no faith in that physician;" or, "I wish I had more faith in Mr. —— as an honest man." So of statements, doctrines, systems, we speak of believing in them, or not believing in them; of full faith in them, or partial faith, or weak faith; and no one misunderstands us.

3. The essential meaning in the Scriptures is the same. There is a difference, however, growing out of the objects on which faith is exercised in the Scriptures, which needs to be noticed. The *objects* of faith, in the Bible, are *moral* or *spiritual*. Faith in its teachings involves *moral consequences*. A statement of facts, in history, in political science, or in physical science, may rest for acceptance simply on the strength of the testimony; and as we have no prepossessions for or against the evidence, or any special interests depending on our acceptance or rejection of the evidence, we yield our minds in a kind of passivity to receive the impressions of said evidence. Here, faith may be said with some propriety to be involuntary. But when that which is offered for our faith involves in its acceptance consequences which may be welcome or unwelcome to us —when it is to result in revolutionizing our principles, our fortune, our life, our destiny, it is evident that other forces, besides the mere testimony, come into play; forces

which dispose us, on the one hand, to receive the testimony eagerly, or on the other, to put it away from us. Here we begin to assert control over our faith, by examining or refusing to examine the evidence; by receiving it in its honest import, or by perverting it from its true meaning. Now the faith of the Gospel does involve tremendous consequences to the sinner. Evil passions, therefore, may step in to pervert the evidence or to prevent its being heard at all. He who believes has exercised his will in hushing adverse pleadings of passion and interest; has asserted his moral powers in determining on an honest attention to the claims of the Gospel. There is, therefore, a moral as well as an intellectual aspect of faith. Intellectually viewed, it is the belief of testimony; morally viewed, it is such a belief of testimony as allows it all its legitimate results over conscience, heart, and life. Hence the Scriptures speak with peculiar emphasis of *believing with the heart*, because a reliance on the truth concerning Jesus calls for the consent and co-operation of the moral nature. Hence, too, in the Gospel, faith is joined with some practical test which compels it out of the limits of mere intellections into the shape and power of a thorough conviction, before it will be accepted. It is joined with repentance, with confession, with baptism, with calling on the name of the Lord—so that it must have its seat in the moral as well as in the intellectual nature before it is recognized as acceptable faith. This does not alter the meaning of the word at all; but it gives it a special hue, derived from the moral objects on which faith is exercised, and the moral results which faith is to produce, which we felt it important to note, lest any of our readers should receive the impression that we are contending for a cold intellectual assent to truth as filling the measure of Scriptural faith. Yet we say that faith means, in the Scriptures, essentially, what it means in its conventional use, whether in the ancient Greek classics or in modern English classics; namely, persuasion, trust, confidence, firm, and earnest belief; the difference in religious faith being found in the nature of the objects on which it rests.

Let us see, now, what the Scriptures affirm.

"Now faith is confidence with respect to things hoped for, persuasion with respect to things not seen."—*Heb. xi.* 1, *Anderson's Trans.*

Abraham's faith is thus described: "Being fully persuaded that what God had promised he was able also to perform."—Rom. iv. 21.

The faith of the Centurion (Matt. viii. 5-10), of which Jesus said, "I have not found so great faith, no, not in Israel," was simply such an unlimited trust in the Savior's power to heal, that speaking the word at a distance, would be as immediately effective as his personal presence.

The faith of the diseased woman (Matt. ix. 20–22), and of the Syro-Phenician woman (Matt. xv. 28), and the examples of approved faith furnished in Heb. xi., all lead to the same conclusion: that faith is persuasion of or reliance on a thing as true; and that faith in Christ is a persuasion that what he promises, he is able to perform.

As we rise above the animal nature, with its instincts and appetites, to a higher plane of being, *faith* is the basis of all excellence. In the earliest dawn of intellectual existence, what inspires and rules the child? Faith. It trusts before it reasons. And it would trust evermore, were it not cruelly assailed by falsehood and deceit, shattering its beautiful and simple faith, and compelling doubt and distrust at every step. So far is it from being true that faith is an arbitrary thing. When God asks men to believe, therefore, he is simply seeking to restore them to the primitive integrity of their nature. Faith is the substance—the foundation—of the dignity of individual life, of the order and security of the social structure, and of civil government. What would man be, were his power to believe annihilated? Without a brute's infallible instincts, with senses much feebler and less acute than belong to inferior animals, shut up within the narrow domain of sensation, and reasoning only upon his sensations, he must necessarily degenerate into the lowest barbarism. His power to rise depends on his power to believe. Faith unlocks to him the experience of the past, the stores of human knowledge and wisdom, the treasures of matter and of mind, puts him into fellowship with the invisible and the real, and pours into his soul the inspirations of history, philosophy, poetry and religion. What is the bond of the family? Faith. Destroy the faith of husband and wife, parent and child, in each other—and does it need fire and brimstone to constitute a hell? What holds society together? The faith of man in man. Read Macaulay's description of the state of society in England about the time of the abdication of James II., when men's faith in government and in each other was almost annihilated, and say what human society would be, destitute of faith? In a despotism, faith in the ruler alone can make such a government tolerable; in a popular government like ours, the faith of man in his fellow-man, and in the government which embodies the popular will, is all that binds the nation in permanent peace and prosperity. And in the business of every day life—what impels the ceaseless activities of commerce, but the faith of man in man? And in the patient toils of the husbandmen—they who are really the substratum of all a nation's prosperity and power—what gives him courage to plow and sow? His faith in God, and in the established order of things.

Now, is it strange or arbitrary, that God should address this faculty of our nature, so wide in the scope of its exercise, so essential to the dignity of the individual character and the peace and order of society, that which is and must ever be the *substance*—the foundation of peace, good government, intellectual growth, and moral greatness; is it strange, we ask, that God should make his appeal to this particular capacity, and constitute this the substance of religious life also? It is not only not strange, but we had almost written that our Creator was shut up in a necessity so to deal with a nature which possesses no other principle so universal in scope, so powerful in acting, so easy of exercise, as the faith-principle.

Faith deals more readily with the concrete than with the abstract. Doctrines and principles are not so appreciable by it until they are embodied in *a person*. The hero-worship of the world, so all-conquering in its enthusiasms, shows how faith rests on a person, and seeks through a person its mightiest inspirations. How adapted to our wants, therefore, the religion which offers as the basis of all our faith, hope, and love, a person—in whom are all the treasures of wisdom, knowledge, power, holiness, goodness, mercy and compassion—all the fullness of the Godhead, and all the wants, woes, and experiences of our manhood! To be a Christian is not to *reason* on the *problems* of foreknowledge, fate, necessity, trinity in unity, or human depravity; but to *believe on the Son of God.* Satan, for aught we know, may be infallibly correct in his knowledge and philosophy of the foregoing and kindred subjects—but that does not save him. "Believe on the Lord Jesus Christ, and thou shalt be saved."

If Jesus of Nazareth is what he professed to be, it needs no labored argument to prove that the highest honor and happiness of man depend on accepting Him in His mission of mercy, and submitting with implicit trust to His guidance. In these matters we *must* walk by faith, or wander in darkness. We see not God; we know not his intentions toward us; we see not heaven; we know not the connection, if any, between this life and the next. Reason has tried in vain for six thousand years to penetrate the mystery. Jesus comes, not to reason, but to testify; to speak what he knows, and testify what he has seen. He sustains his message of supernatural wisdom and knowledge by deeds of supernatural power, and a character of supernatural excellence. He is just what he ought to be, his mission being true. His proofs are just the proofs we would demand of any one who would put us beyond doubt. His teachings are just what our inmost hearts and consciences tell us *must* have come from God. If I can trust my life to a physician on any human evidences of skill, and believe him so implicitly as to go according to his directions, believing where I do not comprehend; if I can trust my earthly destiny, in faith, to the navigator, with only a plank between me and destruction, on the evidence of his ability to guide me safely over the treacherous deep; then may I, for better reasons and on better evidence, resign my entire being to the control and guidance of the Lord Jesus, as being able to save unto the uttermost all who come to God by him.

We have in these remarks anticipated what we desired to say as to the sources of faith. It will be at once apparent that faith in Jesus can only flow from a knowledge of his character, his teaching, and his works. It must come, therefore, through the Bible which contains the record of these. See John xx. 31; Acts xvii. 12; Rom. x. 17.

We are sometimes asked if the evidences of the truth concerning Jesus are as full and indisputable as they can be? We answer, no. We can easily conceive how the evidence could be made more abundant and demonstrative than it is. We can see how it might be made so completely a matter of demonstration that it could not be resisted —so as to leave no election to us whether to believe or not. But the moment that was done all the *moral* element of faith would be eliminated. It would no longer be *our* act—the *choice* of our hearts; and it could, of course, serve none of the moral purposes in regeneration which it is now designed to serve. As it is, the evidence is sufficient to lead the honest heart, that seeks for truth as for silver, to find it; and yet it is not so overwhelming, nor so free from objection, that a dishonest or unwilling heart may not evade its claims and continue in unbelief. He, therefore, who rejects the evidences on which this religion now rests might be silenced, but would not be converted, by any additional evidence. Hence, said Jesus, "If they believe not Moses and the prophets, neither would they believe though one rose from the dead."

Have a care, my dear sir, that you come not under the condemnation of unbelief.

LETTER XII.

Repentance defined and illustrated.

Intimately and inseparably associated with Faith as a condition of salvation, is the command to *repent.* "God commandeth all men everywhere to repent." Acts xvii. 30. "Repentance and remission of sins shall be preached in his name, among all nations, beginning at Jerusalem." Luke xxiv. 47. As the special work of the Harbinger, in preparing a people for the Lord, was to call the Jews to repentance, we may well understand that none can be made ready for the reign of the Lord Messiah except as they repent. Let us, then, inquire what is meant by repentance?

Metanoëo, translated repent, means *to come to a conviction afterward;* hence *to change one's mind or purpose.* In Scripture usage, it signifies sometimes to undergo a change in frame of mind and feeling, and sometimes, a change of principle and practice. Indeed, this latter, though not always expressed, is generally implied. Perhaps no better definition can be given than is furnished in the Standards of the Church in which you were educated. "True repentance includes a turning from sin unto God, with a sincere purpose and endeavor to walk with him in all the ways of his commandments." It is not mere sorrow for sin, for we read of "sorrowing unto repentance." And we are taught that "godly sorrow worketh repentance unto salvation." 2 Cor. vii. 10. Neither is it actual reformation, as we generally understand that term, only in its *initiative* stage; for Paul assures us that he taught both Jews and Greeks that they should "repent and turn to God, and do works meet for repentance." Acts xxvi. 20. Repentance, then, is that which succeeds godly sorrow and precedes the external fruits of reformation. This can be nothing but the *change of will or purpose*—the renunciation of sin and the acceptance, in heart and intention, of the law of God as the rule of life. This explains the use of the term Acts ii. 38. They were commanded to repent, *after* they were "cut to the heart," proving that even the most poignant sorrow did not of itself constitute repentance. And they were accepted as penitents before they began a new life, any farther than their baptism indicated the entrance on a new life. Their repentance was the renunciation of sin and the acceptance of Christ as their Lord and Savior *in the purpose of their hearts;* and their baptism was the expression of this renunciation, and the beginning of this new life of obedience to Christ. As the process stands revealed to us, thus far, it is, 1. Faith. 2. Godly sorrow. 3. Repentance or the internal submission to Christ. 4. Turning to God, or Baptism—the external turning to God. 5. Works meet for repentance.

We may be allowed to quote yet farther from your former standards in regard to the place which repentance occupies in the order of the Gospel.

"With regard to the *order* of faith and repentance, it may be remarked that we can form no conception of a moment of time when the one exists in the soul separate from the other. In point of *time*, then, faith and repentance necessarily accompany each other; but in the order of *nature*, faith must precede repentance. Evangelical repentance is a turning from sin to God; but there can be no turning to God, except through Christ; and no coming to Christ, but by believing in him. John xiv. 6 : vi. 35.

Besides, evangelical repentance flows from love to God; but the exercise of unfeigned love to him proceeds from the exercise of true faith. 1 Tim. i. 5. Add to this, it is only by looking on him whom we have pierced, that we can mourn after a godly sort, according to that remarkable promise. "They shall look on me whom they have pierced, and they shall mourn for him." Zech. xii. 10. There is indeed a conviction of the person's guilt and misery, accompanied with a kind of sorrow for sin, and resolutions to forsake it, because it exposes him to everlasting punishment, which in the nature of things must precede the exercise of faith in Christ; but this is very different from evangelical repentance." —Exp. of Conf., p. 181.

You cannot but see that this condition of salvation is not arbitrarily imposed. In the very nature of things, repentance *must* take place before Gospel blessings can be enjoyed. As well expect a man to see the sun with his face buried in the sand, or to taste an orange by touching it with the tips of his fingers; as well expect an untamed Indian to be at home in a circle of highly refined *literati*, or a drunkard reeking with the fumes of the bar-room to be supremely happy in a prayer-meeting, as to expect an impenitent man to enjoy the blessings of the salvation of God. For what does the Gospel propose? To bring us to purity, to righteousness, and to love—and in and through these to fellowship with God. Unquestionably, then, if the heart is sold to sin, and all the powers of the moral nature are under the control of selfishness, there can be no access to the blessings of salvation, except by such a repentance as shall revolutionize the desires, intents, and purposes of the heart. Only the pure can have fellowship with the pure—the best of all reasons why the impenitent cannot receive the Holy Spirit.

This repentance is something *that we must accomplish.* In its very essence, it is the assertion of self-sovereignty, the exercise of will in a new direction. Hence we are *commanded* to repent. The obligation lies on us to repent. True, God is spoken of as *granting* repentance: but he grants repentance by granting the *means* of repentance, and by granting us assurance of acceptance when we do repent. The *motives* to repentance are, (1) the goodness of God; (Rom. ii. 4); and (2) the coming righteous judgment. (Acts xvii. 31). The soul stands between the divine charms of the one and the divine terrors of the other, to be at once moved and urged—charmed and warned into a new life, in view of the tremendous issues of an impenitent course of conduct. These motives God reveals and urges; but the choice—the decision—is our own.

Many are distressed for want of evidence of a *change of heart.* It would help them much to drop that phraseology and the ideas it has carried, and ask instead for the evidence of *faith* and *repentance.* When our *affections* and *desires* are purified from sin, and our *principles* and *purposes* are changed so as to renounce that which is sinful, and choose that which is good, there can be no reasonable question that the heart is changed. Faith and repentance accomplish this revolution.

Let us add, in conclusion, that the necessity for repentance being laid in the eternal law of God—in the nature of things—there can be no compromise in regard to it. The sinner *must* repent or perish. At whatever cost, the right eye that offends must be plucked out, the right hand or foot that offends must be cut off, and we must go maimed into life, or, failing in this sacrifice, must be cast into hell-fire. This more than any intellectual embarrassment, is the offense of the Gospel; yet to every heart capable of appreciating the good and the true, this will be one of its most satisfactory recommendations.

Letter from an Inquirer.—III.

Mr Editor:—I am willing to admit that your late numbers on Faith and Repentance have done much to remove doubt, by showing that they are not arbitrary conditions, imposed by mere authority; and are ordained because *in the nature of things* they are essential to the reception and enjoyment of salvation. Can you prove the same of Baptism? This, in your arrangement, will come next in order. How can you make a mere rite anything else than arbitrary? And why should we have all this controversy over a mere form, as if it could be of any value, or as if it could possibly affect a man's salvation whether he is sprinkled, poured or immersed? Pardon me if I seem uncivil in saying that this looks to me very much like straining at a gnat. Better attend to the "weightier matters of the law" of which you speak so forcibly in an editorial of the 27th.

An Inquirer.

LETTER XIII.

Baptism not a mere arbitrary appointment—Reason for such an Ordinance—Its importance.

I am convinced that too much has been yielded in admitting that baptism has no fitness — no foundation in the nature of things; that it is a purely arbitrary appointment. The distinction which theological writers make between the Positive-Moral, and Moral-Positive, may be convenient for some purposes, and may, from a particular angle of vision, express a true difference. But it is not a Scriptural distinction, and I am quite sure that too much has been made of it. Baptism is *not* an arbitrary appointment. It is made to rest on authority more than the other conditions mentioned, because it is in its design, an acknowledgement and recognition of authority; and for this purpose it has fitness, for the very reason that it is destitute of the moral qualities which belong to the previously named conditions, and brings us more directly face to face with the sovereign authority of the Lord Jesus. But it is false to say that it lacks adaptedness to its purpose, or that a necessity for it is not found in the nature of things. Let us see.

1. The design of the Founder of Christianity was to establish *a society;* not merely to convert individuals from sin and wrong,

and to plant the seeds of a new life in individual hearts—but to unite the converts in an association for mutual help, and as an instrumentality for the conversion of others. Thus there are public and social as well as personal and private ends to be served by becoming a Christian. This society is called the Church. It is an organized body. It must have conditions of membership, and a form of initiation. As it is a visible society, made up of men and women in the body, and having only public objects to accomplish, the mode of initiation must be visible, tangible, and public, so that the church and the world may know the line of separation, and who stands on this side and who on that. That there should be, therefore, a visible form of initiation into the Church, is a necessity. *This* is not arbitrary.

2. Moreover, such a rite being necessary to subserve the ends of this society called the Church, it is fitting that the rite of initiation be expressive of the life to which it leads, and of the faith and purposes of those who submit to it. Every society, therefore, seeks in its modes of initiation that which will express in symbol, its principles and aims, or that which will impress on the subject just ideas of the obligations which he assumes. For this reason one form is not equal to another. Mere authority cannot make one form as good as another. The *fitness of things* requires that that form shall be

chosen—that symbol adopted—which will most clearly embody and express the reigning ideas and characteristics of the life to which it leads. Hence a baptism in blood, or in pitch, or in oil, could not serve the purpose of initiation into the Christian life as baptism in *water* does. Because it is an entrance on a life of *purity*—a renunciation of a life of sin; and the cleansing element of water alone can give this adequate expression. The *separation* from the world which this ordinance expresses, could in no other form be so well expressed, as in *the burial* of the subject as being already dead to sin—cut off from all sympathy with and participation in it. The *new life* to which he gives himself finds its best expression in *resurrection* from the symbolical grave. And the *entireness* of the consecration of his whole nature to a new service has no such fitting symbol as the total immersion of the whole man in pure water, and his emersion from that element as one who has been washed and cleansed, and has arisen from his old defilements to a life of holiness. *This* is not arbitrary.

3. Religion is not a mere intellection, nor a mere sentiment, but *a life*. Its object is to teach us how to live. Hence its promises of salvation are not made to us until our convictions and desires come out into life. In fact, faith is not stamped as faith, repentance is not accepted as repentance until it

lives and moves in definite obedience to the will of God. Hence an external act is associated with the internal conviction, in the Gospel conditions. "He that believeth *and is baptized* shall be saved." "Repent *and be baptized*, in the name of Jesus Christ for the remission of sins." "Repent *and turn*, that your sins may be blotted out." Baptism is, therefore, but faith and repentance, brought out of doors—translated into the language of life. If this were appreciated it would prevent a great deal of harping on a class of texts where faith is spoken of without adjuncts, or in opposition to justification by law. It is, in all these cases, contemplated, not merely as an internal conviction, but as a *living principle*—faith translated into obedience. There is certainly a fitness in meeting with pardon, at the threshold of life, when in the very fact of emerging into a life of obedience, the sinner whom God would forgive in order that he may live a life of faithfulness. The truth is that we never know ourselves, whether we are really wedded to a cause until we commit ourselves to it in definite act, which cannot be honorably recalled. We may stand on the brink of the Rubicon, and believe, and resolve, and wish, and promise, and yet never enter. It is *the crossing of the Rubicon* that settles the question. Would the American Revolution ever have been proceeded with through all its disasters and despairs, had not the Declaration of Independence been *signed*, and its signers thus openly pledged to all its consequences? Is there no meaning in a soldier's act of enlistment? none in the ordinance of marriage? none in the act of naturalization? In all these we recognize the principle which we have mentioned—the necessity of associating external consecration, with internal conviction, in cases where *a new life* is the end that is sought. THIS is not arbitrary.

4. We have a material organism. The soul is reached through the avenues of sense. The soul also puts forth its power through the physical organization. It needs, therefore, in harmony with this organization, sensible tests—tangible evidences—and, in a great crisis of life, such as conversion, definite external acts of consecration, which will not only satisfy a present want, but enable Memory, by the power of association, to erect a landmark in the wilderness of life. Call this weakness if you will. We doubt not that ordinances, as enjoined on us, are a merciful condescension to our weakness. Pure spirits may not need ordinances; but men in the flesh do need them. Even Abraham, with the promise of Jehovah sounding in his ears that the land of Canaan should be his, had to ask, in the weakness of his nature, "Whereby *shall I know* that I shall inherit it?" Not until the altar was built, the sacrifices divided in twain, and the

Shekinah had met him between the divided parts, in solemn ratification of the covenant, did he *know* that he should inherit the land. God does not need ordinances—but man needs them. Many are startled that in this nineteenth century, we should witness a backward march into the ritualism of the dark ages. But it at least shows that there is something in human nature that seeks the aid of sensuous media of communication with the spiritual. All the boasted light of Rationalism cannot prevent it. And in the end we shall witness the spectacle of men who have forsworn all forms and rites plunging into all the blind excesses of Ritualism, to escape from the dreary and unbearable isolation into which the formless and godless theories of Rationalism had led them.

That this tendency of our nature can be and has been terribly perverted, is beyond question. But not in the New Testament. The Gospel has few forms, few and simple ordinances. It is pre-eminently a spiritual religion; yet one of the proofs of its divine origin is, that while seeking the highest spiritual ends, it does not ignore, but regulates, the craving of our nature for the external aid of ordinances.

There is, therefore, nothing superstitious, nothing irrational, in Scriptural baptism. It is adapted to the wants of our being, and to the needs of the Church and of the world. Its just significance may, in the light of what has been said, be learned from a few considerations.

1. *It is initiatory.* It is, therefore, one of those germinal acts which has in it all of the life that is to be: an act whose meaning is never exhausted while life lasts. It is impossible to express in words the solemnity and sublimity of an act which gives away a life and a destiny so that it can never, in honor, be recalled.

2. *It is, therefore, to be performed but once.* An act that is to be performed but once in a lifetime has, for that very reason, peculiar significance and interest. It ought, of all acts, to be the most deliberate, and accurate in form as well as in spirit; and should be performed in such intelligence, sincerity, and devotion, as may make it to us, living and dying, a bright, and fragrant, and blessed memory.

3. *Its office is to change our spiritual relationships.* The use of the preposition *eis* in connection with it is quite significant. This preposition is indicative of motion toward, to, on, or into. And when we read, "Baptizing them *into* the name of the Father, and of the Son, and of the Holy Spirit;" "baptized into Christ;" "baptized *into* his death;" it is the clearest expression of its intention to bring the subject into new relations to the Godhead, and to identify him with Christ and his death, as a personal participant in the blessings of the great salvation.

4. It is the only act with which are associated the names of Father, Son, and Holy Spirit. The glory and the benedictions of the Godhead rest on this ordinance as on no other—for in the peculiar place it occupies, it brings us face to face with Deity, in the threefold manifestations of Father, Son, and Spirit, and establishes new and permanent relations with the Father as *our* Father, with the Son as *our* Brother and Redeemer, with the Holy Spirit as *our* Comforter, the earnest of *our* inheritance.

While, then, there is no reason in the Scriptures for our enslavement to burdensome forms, there is abundant reason for cheerful submission to an ordinance which meets us in the great crisis of life with the most beautiful adaption to our circumstances and our wants.

LETTER XIV.

A change of state.

Having vindicated the ordinance of baptism from the complaint that it is a mere arbitrary rite, and shown the necessity of such a rite to associate the external with the internal, and to be to ourselves as well as to others an evidence of our actual entrance on a new life; we propose to speak more fully, in this number, of its office in effecting a change of state or relationship.

Your attention has been called to the force

of the Greek preposition *eis*, as indicating motion out of one place or state into another. Our preposition *into* is, when it is used in this sense, its fair equivalent. We constantly use it to denote the transition from one state to another: "Sworn *into* office;" "Mustered *into* service;" "Married *into* the family," etc. We understand by this that the appointed oath, marriage ceremony, or whatever else is spoken of in such phraseology, effected a transition of the parties out of one state into another. Before the oath was taken, the person did not occupy the office, immediately on taking it he did occupy it. Before the process of enlistment was gone through with, the man was not a soldier in the service of the State—could not perform the duties nor claim the rights of a soldier; immediately on its completion all a soldier's duties, obligations, rights, and privileges were his. Before the marriage ceremony is performed, the man is not a husband—the woman is not a wife; her name, her fortune, her right to dispose of herself, are still her own; but the moment the ordinance of marriage is obeyed, the relations of the parties are changed; life-long obligations rest on them which, a moment before, were not yet assumed, and consequences involving name, fortune, home, and all that makes up earthly life and destiny, result from submission to that one ordinance. *There are no degrees in state.* A person is either married or unmarried; a citizen or an alien; in office or out of office. The preparation for this new state may be gradual, but the change of state is instantaneous. And thus so far as state is concerned, a man is a Christian or not a Christian; a citizen of the kingdom or an alien; a member of God's family or a stranger, justified or condemned; reconciled or unreconciled; sanctified or unsanctified; saved or lost. The *preparation* for citizenship, for justification, for adoption, may be gradual. Faith and repentance involve this preparation. But the actual entrance on the new state is the work of a moment.

Let us call your attention, just here, to a very significant passage of Scripture. "Wherefore remember * * * that *at that time* ye were *without Christ*, being *aliens* from the commonwealth of Israel, and *strangers* from the covenants of promise, *having no hope*, and *without God in the world*. But *now*, *in* Christ Jesus, ye who were *formerly* far off are made nigh by the blood of Christ. * * * *Now*, therefore, ye are no more strangers and foreigners, but *fellow-citizens* with the saints, and of the household of God." Eph. ii. 11–22. Here, most evidently there is described *a change of state;* not merely a change of disposition and character, but a change of relationship. They *had been* aliens—they were *now* citizens; they *had been* strangers—they were *now* members of the household; they *had been* out of Christ—they were now *in* Christ Jesus. *There was a moment and an act in which that change had been effected.*

Take another text. "Wherefore, my brethren, ye also are become dead to the law by the body of Christ, *that ye should be married to another*, even to him who is raised from the dead, that we should bring forth fruit unto God. For when we were *in the flesh* [under the law] the motions of sins, which were by the law, did work in our members to bring forth fruit unto death. But *now* we are delivered from the law, that being dead wherein we were held, that we should serve in newness of the spirit and not in the oldness of the letter." Rom. vii. 4–6. Here again is described a *change of state*—a marriage to Christ of these believers. There was a time, then, when they were unmarried—an act by which they were married—and a moment in which that act took them out of their uncovenanted state and brought them into the marriage covenant.

Again: "Salute Andronicus and Junia, my kinsmen, and my fellow-prisoners, who are of note among the apostles; *who also were in Christ before me.*" Rom. xvi. 7.

Yet again: "Who hath delivered us from the power of darkness, *and hath translated us into the kingdom of his dear Son.*" Col. i. 13.

Now under whatever imagery we regard this new state to which the Gospel invites us—as a kingdom, a family, a church, a body or a covenant, we are introduced into it by that initiatory act called baptism. Is it a kingdom? We "enter into the kingdom" by being *born of water* and of the Spirit. John iii. 5. Is it a church? "Then they that gladly received the word were baptized, and the same day were added to them about three thousand souls." Acts ii. 41. Is it a body? "In one Spirit are we all baptized into one body." 1 Cor. xii. 13. Is it a covenant? Those who were "strangers from the covenants of promise" are made children of the covenant "in Christ," by being "baptized into Christ." Is it a family? "Ye are all the children of God by faith in Christ Jesus, for as many as have been baptized into Christ have put on Christ." Gal. iii. 26, 27.

Hence whatever blessings are in the covenant—in citizenship—in adoption—in marriage to Christ—to all these blessings baptism brings us, since baptism is the consummation of the process of conversion, and the solemn act which brings us into covenant relationship to God. There is no need for so much verbal criticism on the passages which declare baptism to be "for the remission of sins." It does not rest on the precise rendering of a preposition in two or three texts. For when it is established that baptism is *initiatory*—that it changes our state—it is settled beyond reach of cavil that it conducts us to the remission of sins and to all other covenant mercies. Is remission of sins a covenant blessing? Most certainly. See Heb. viii. 13. Then, if baptism brings us into covenant, baptism is certainly for remission of sins. If reconciliation, justification, adoption, sanctification, describe, in different phases, the Gospel state, then all the blessings described in these various terms come to us through baptism as the ordinance which brings us into this state.

But let it not be forgotten, in all this, that baptism has no significance except *as an act of faith*—as an act of self-consecration. It has no meaning otherwise. But more of this when we come to speak of the subjects of this ordinance.

Let us ask you, my dear sir, to dismiss the rationalistic cant about slavish forms, and ask yourself whether you are in Christ or out of Christ—a stranger or a child of God—an alien or a citizen of the kingdom? On the one side all is bankruptcy and ruin—on the other are "righteousness, peace, and joy in the Holy Spirit."

Permit us to say, in concluding this paper, that there is no such difference of sentiment over the design of baptism as many think. The great majority of the Christian world, of all ages, give it the full significance with which this essay clothes it. The difference is, that through the prevalence of infant membership, the ordinance has come to have, *in itself*, the meaning which the Scriptures only assign it *as an act of faith.* While it has been degraded into a mere ceremony, there is still claimed for it all the virtue and efficacy of an act of self-consecration to God.

LETTER XV.

What is Baptism?—Sophistry covered up by the phrase "modes of baptism"—the Literal, Metaphorical, and Symbolical uses of the word.

In treating of what is generally termed the "mode of baptism," we are well aware that to persons of rationalistic tendencies it seems a very trifling discussion—a dispute over a mere form. It certainly is a cause of regret that there should be so protracted a controversy over such a question; but since the necessity is on us of vindicating the integrity of a divine ordinance, we desire to say, in answer to your objections,

1. That in view of what we have already developed of the design of baptism, it is an ordinance in which we publicly acknowledge the supreme authority of the Lord Jesus, and disown all other spiritual lordships. The language of the candidate for baptism is, "I renounce all self-will and all other wills, and desire only to know and do the will of the Lord Jesus." Evidently, therefore, the only inquiry here is, "Lord, what wilt *thou* have me to do?" The very object of baptism is defeated if the will of

the candidate or the will of a religious sect is substituted for the will of our only Lord and Savior. If men wish to be baptized "in the name"—by the authority—of a human leader or of a sect, let the will of that leader or sect be consulted as to the mode of initiation; but as long as we desire to be baptized "in the name of Jesus Christ," *His* will must settle the question.

2. The ordinances of the Gospel are few. It is worth while to keep them as they were given. If there were no direct authority involved in settling the question, there would still be a propriety in observing them as they were delivered. "Now I praise you, brethren, that ye remember me in all things, *and keep the ordinances as I delivered them to you.*" 1 Cor. xi. 2. And if this is a just occasion of praise, it is a just occasion of censure when the ordinances are not kept as they were delivered. Hence, when, in the same chapter, the apostle points out their perversion of the Lord's Supper, he says, "I praise you not." Moreover, if it is important that all the ordinances be kept "as they were delivered," there is a special reason for accuracy in the case of baptism, since it can rightfully be observed but once; and if worth attending to at all, it is worth attending to with the utmost precision, so that one need never afterward be distressed with doubts or burdened with regrets.

We ask, then, *What is baptism?* What is

that act which we thus designate? We are told that sprinkling, pouring, and immersion are "modes of baptism." If this be so, we ask, *What is that thing of which these are modes?* Let baptism itself be defined. We are not now speaking of Christian baptism — but baptism back of all modes and all special appropriations. We press this question in vain on the advocates of sprinkling and pouring. The sophistry of their arguments about the "modes" appears the moment you press them for a definition of the word itself. Surely, if there are modes of baptism, the baptism itself is one thing, and the modes another. And certainly the act called baptism can be defined. It cannot be that our Lord has chosen as descriptive of the initiating act in his religion, a word which is incapable of definition. It is not to be easily believed that he would choose a word whose meaning was not definite and unmistakable. We have no difficulty in defining the term. We say that it means immersion. We are willing to test this definition in all the uses of the word, classical and Scriptural—literal, metaphorical, poetical, or symbolical. And when it is denied that this is a correct definition, we demand that those who find fault with it shall furnish a better. We press on them the question—not what are the modes of baptism, but—What is baptism? Tell us the meaning of the word. Every attempt to meet this demand will reveal the weakness and sophistry of the advocates of rantism.

Sometimes we are told that baptism is "the application of water in the name of the Father, Son, and Holy Ghost." But this will not do, for water has no necessary association with baptism. It has a necessary association with *Christian* baptism. But we are seeking a definition of the word, without adjuncts. The word was in use before the Christian ordinance was established. What did it mean? That it did not mean "the application of water," is evident from the fact that it is used when water has no association with it; as, for instance, the baptism in the Holy Spirit—in fire—in sufferings. There may be a baptism in blood—in oil—in wine—in any liquid.

Again, we are told, it means to wash—to purify. Now, metonymically, in its *Christian* application, it may mean to wash; but this does not define the term: for it would not do to say that a person was washed in fire, or washed in a mire!

It is argued, we are aware, that the New Testament sense of the word is different from its classical sense. This is possible. But it must have had a classical meaning at the time it was appropriated to a special use in the New Testament. And when that meaning is found, there will be discovered, in that meaning, some reasonable ground for the sense in which it was appropriated in the Gospel. So again we press the demand—*define the word.* If sprinkling is a *mode* of baptism, then sprinkling does not define the action. So of pouring. So of immersion. Let the action itself be defined. We are anxious to see the anti-immersionists undertake it.

We have said that baptism means *immersion.* We propose, in this letter, to test this definition. We must necessarily condense our statements of fact, which cover too much ground to be given in detail. And as we write for popular use, we cannot enter largely into learned criticisms. We must give results, rather than the processes by which they have been reached. Yet if, in attempting this necessary condensation, we furnish statements and conclusions that do not seem to our readers to be supported by sufficient testimony, we have only to say that we are responsible for the statements we make, and will be forthcoming with proofs whenever these statements are challenged.

I. As we are treating of a Greek word, it is proper first to inquire into its classical use. That the Greek lexicons generally give *to dip, plunge, immerse,* as its literal and primary signification, is a fact beyond question. We could fill columns with testimonies to this point. But at present we refer to the standard Greek-English lexicon of the present time—Liddell & Scott's. We subjoin a statement of the plan on which this lexicon was constructed:

> "Our plan has been that marked out and begun by Passow, viz: *to make each Article a History of the usage of the word referred to.* That is, we have always sought to give the earliest authority for its use first. Then, if no change was introduced by later writers, we have left it with that early authority alone—adding, however, whether it continued in general use or no, and taking care to specify whether it was common to Prose and Poetry, or confined to one only. In most cases the word will tell its own story; the passages quoted will themselves say whether it continued in use, and whether it was used or no both in Poetry and Prose; for there are few words that do not change their signification more or less in the downward course of Time, and few, therefore, that do not need many references.—*Preface*, p. xx.

It is very instructive to trace, in a lexicon on this plan, the changes in the meaning of words, often very numerous and subtle. But it is remarkable that in the case of *baptizo*, there is no such history of change. It is given, "1. *To dip repeatedly;* of ships, *to sink* them. Pass. *To bathe; soaked in wine; over head and ears in debt;* a boy *drowned* with questions. 2. *To draw water.* 3. *To baptize.* N. T. Hence, *Baptisis*, a dipping, bathing, drawing water, baptism. *Baptisma*, that which is dipped."

In the first edition of this lexicon, we believe that wash, pour, and sprinkle, were included among the meanings of this word; but in subsequent editions they were dropped as unworthy to stand the test of classical usage.

From Dr. Conant's treatise on *baptizein*, we give the summing up, after a full examination of all the lexical and grammatical uses of it:

"1. From the preceding examples it appears that the ground-idea expressed by this word is, *to put into or under water* (or other penetrable substances), so as entirely *to immerse* or *submerge*; that this act is always expressed in the literal application of the word, and is the basis of the metaphorical uses. This ground idea is expressed in English, in the various connections where the word occurs, by the terms (synonymous in this ground-element) *to immerse, immerge, submerge, to dip, to plunge, to imbathe, to whelm.*

"2. These examples are drawn from writers in almost every department of literature and science; from poets, rhetoricians, philosophers, critics, historians, geographers; from writers on husbandry, on medicine, on natural history, on grammer, on theology; from almost every form and style of composition, romances, epistles, orations, fables, odes, epigrams, sermons, narratives; from writers of various nations and religions, Pagan, Jew and Christian, belonging to many different countries, and through a long succession of ages.

"3. In all, the word has retained its ground-meaning, without change. From the earliest age of Greek literature down to its close (a period of about two thousand years), not an example has been found in which the word has any other meaning. There is no instance in which it signifies to make a partial application of water by *affusion* or *sprinkling*, or *to cleanse, to purify*, apart from the literal act of immersion as the *means* of cleansing or purifying."—*Meaning and Use of Baptizein*, p. 58.

Let us see, then, whether this ground-idea is retained in New Testament usage. We will look at some examples of the various uses of the word, literal, metaphorical, symbolical.

II.—In *law*, in giving commands, or asserting authority, we look for words to be used in their literal sense, unless it involves an absurdity, or there is something in the context to require another meaning to be assigned to them. Hence, when we read, "Go teach all nations, *baptizing* them," etc.; "He that believeth and is *baptized* shall be saved;" "Repent and be *baptized*, every one of you;" "Arise, and be *baptized*, and wash away thy sins," etc.; we naturally seek the literal meaning of the word, and read, "Go, teach all nations, *immersing* them." "He that believeth and is *immersed* shall be saved." "Repent and be *immersed* every one of you." "Arise and be *immersed*." This certainly involves no absurdity. Nor is there anything in the context requiring a departure from the literal meaning of the word. True, we are told that three thousand could not be immersed in one day; and that there was not water in Jerusalem to immerse them in. But this is mere caviling. For, 1. Enough baptizers could be delegated by the apostles from the one hundred and twenty disciples to immerse three thousand leisurely and becomingly in a very few hours; and, 2. Wherever people can live, water can be had for such purpose—certainly in a city with immense pools such as Jerusalem had, and with a temple service that required large supplies of water. The literal meaning of the word makes good sense, in its preceptive form, for *persons* can be immersed; while the command to sprinkle, or to pour, must relate to the *water*, and not to the *person*. You sprinkle *water*, pour *water*, but immerse the *person;* and as the *person* and not the *water*, is to be baptized, there is an entire fitness in the literal meaning of the word—while sprinkle or pour requires a usage of the term which, to say the least, is very doubtful.

When we come to the narrative of the obedience rendered to this commandment, every thing favors the literal meaning of the word. Candidates were baptized "*in* water." Matt. iii. 11. We know that the common version says "*with* water;" but there is no good reason for this rendering of the preposition *en*, especially in view of the fact that in the 6th verse the same preposition is rendered *in:* "and were baptized of him *in* Jordan." It would hardly do to say that they were sprinkled or poured *with* the river Jordan! The most eminent pedobaptist critics yield this point. They were baptized, then, *in* the river. John baptized in Enon, "because there was much water there." John iii. 23. Philip and the eunuch "went down both into the water," and "came up out of the water." Acts viii. 38, 39. All this is easy, natural, and perfectly intelligible, in view of immersion; it is language which has to be tortured to compel it into consistency with sprinkling or pouring.

There is indeed a use of the term in Mark vii. 1, 2, 3, and Luke xi. 37, 38, which is supposed to involve the idea of immersion in difficulty. They speak of the baptism of cups, pots, brazen vessels and couches, and of the baptism of persons after returning from market, and before meals. We can not go into a full examination of the texts here. Suffice it to say that neither impossibility nor absurdity is involved in the literal application of the term in these instances. The immersion of cups, pots, and brazen vessels certainly is not absurd; the immersion of couches on which they had reclined, to cleanse them from legal defilement, is in harmony with Jewish teachings, both in the law and in the traditions. Regarding things unclean, the law said: "Every thing that may abide the fire, ye shall make it *go through* the fire, and it shall be clean; nevertheless, it shall be purified with the water of separation: and all that abideth not the fire, ye shall make *go through* the water." Numb. xxxi. 23. "A bed that is wholly defiled," says Maimonides, "if he dips it part by part, it is pure. If he dips the bed in the pool, although the feet are plunged in the deep clay, at the bottom of the pool, it is clean. What shall he do with a pillow or bolster of skin? He must dip them and lift them up by the fringes." Respecting the baptism of persons coming home from market, Dr. Carson has well said,

"If an Egyptian, on touching a swine, would run to the river and plunge in with his clothes, is it strange that superstitious Pharisees should immerse themselves after the pollution of the market?"

No reason, then, appears for departing from the literal meaning of the word in its preceptive and narrative uses, in the New Testament. Scarcely less convincing than classic and scriptural usage and lexical definition, as to the literal meaning of *baptizo*, is the metaphorical use of the word in the New Testament. You know with what frequency and force the word *immerse* is employed metaphorically, to denote the overwhelming abundance of an influence or power; as, immersed in pleasure, immersed in sorrow, immersed in debt, etc. The force of the term when thus employed, is derived from its literal meaning. It carries a meaning which does not and cannot belong to sprinkle or pour, in such a connection. Who would think to express an overwhelming sorrow, by the phrase "sprinkled with sorrow," or even by the phrase, "poured with sorrow?" The incongruity is at once apparent. But you can fully express an overwhelming sorrow by the phrase "immersed in sorrow," because the idea of overwhelming is at once suggested by the word immerse.

1. Now we have just such a metaphorical use of the word baptize, in the New Testa-

ment. The overwhelming sorrow and anguish of the Savior's last sufferings are called a baptism. "Are you able to drink of the cup that I shall drink of, and to be baptized with the baptism that I am baptized with?" Matt. xx. 22. "But I have a baptism to be baptized with, and how am I straitened till it be accomplished?" Luke xii. 50. That the sorrows of the Sufferer were not light, as sprinkling or pouring would suggest, but deep and overpowering we surely do not need to prove. Yet this word *baptism* is chosen to express forcibly their overwhelming power and fullness. Why? No other reason can be given than that the word literally means *immersion.* This at once suggests itself to every reader, and is uniformly admitted even by the stoutest advocates of sprinkling. We subjoin two or three pedobaptist commentaries on this text.

Bengel says: "Baptism, among the Jews, was a thing to be shuddered at, inasmuch as the whole body was dipped into a stream, however cold. Accordingly by both words the passion of Christ is denoted: by *the cup*, his inward passion; the *cup* is therefore placed first; by the *baptism*, chiefly his external passion. He was distended inwardly with his passion (referring to *the cup;* he was *filled* with the cup of anguish); he was *covered over* (as a person baptized is with water) with his passion."—*Gnomon*, Mark x. 38.

Adam Clarke, on Matt. xx. 22, says: "Baptism among the Jews, as it was performed in the coldest weather, and the persons were kept under water for some time, was used not only to express death, but the most cruel kind of death."

"I have indeed a most dreadful baptism to be baptized with, and know that I shall shortly be *bathed*, as it were, in blood, and *plunged* in the most overwhelming distress."—*Doddridge, on Luke* xii. 50.

Dr. Van Oosterzee, in Lange's Commentary, Luke xii. 50, says: "Over against the heavenly fire which he sends, stands the earthly water of the suffering which previously to that *must roll entirely over him. To be baptized*,—An image of the *depth* and *intensity* of this suffering, like a baptism performed by immersion."

These are only specimens of the general style of comment on these texts. It is not for us to say how these men could reconcile these views with their practice of sprinkling for baptism. It is very clear that if the word figuratively means such an utter overwhelming, it can literally mean nothing less than immersion.

2. A second instance of the metaphorical use of the term is found in Matt. iii. 11, and kindred passages. That there was no literal baptism of these persons in the Holy Spirit or in fire, we presume no one will ask us to prove. That the baptism in the Holy Spirit denoted the abundant and overwhelming influence of the Spirit, which Christ was to impart, is generally admitted; and that this was suggested by the literal immersion in water, we have no doubt. The baptism in fire appears to describe, like the baptism of sufferings, a coming calamity, perfectly overwhelming. The chaff was to be burned up in fire; the tares were to be cast into a furnace of fire;—all bold images to denote

the deep and terrible calamities that, like a flood, would sweep over the ungodly. Great stress is laid by affusionists on the fact that the Spirit was to be "*poured out*," and strong efforts are made to press this phrase into the service, as if it was used on purpose to denote the mode of baptism. This, however, is unworthy of serious consideration. The pouring and the immersion are alike figurative when applied to the mission of the Spirit. Pouring out, we presume, is employed to denote that the Spirit was to *descend* from heaven; and immersion to denote the abundance of the gift bestowed. In all this there is fitness and beauty, and nothing but a blind, partisan spirit would ever seek to disturb or mar it. Listen to Dr. Lechler, the translator and commentator of Acts, in Lange's splendid series:

> "*Baptized with the Holy Ghost.*—The gift of the Spirit is here termed a *Baptism*, and is thus characterized as one of *the most abundant fullness*, and as a *submersion* in a purifying and life-giving element. The term and the image are both derived from the water-baptism of John."

This, too, is furnished merely as a *specimen* of the comment of men of candor and learning, and who are happily far removed from the belittling and perverting influences that surround, as with an atmosphere, the denominational pettifogger. We could fill much space with equally candid testimonies, but deem it unnecessary. We pass on to consider

The *symbolical* use of the word. That it should have a symbolical sense, we would at once suppose, on learning that it belongs to an initiatory rite. It is customary to give a symbolical significance to rites of initiation. Let us read, then, Rom. vi. 3, 4.

"Know ye not that so many of us as were baptized into Jesus Christ were baptized into his death? Therefore we are buried with him by baptism into death, that like as Christ was raised from the dead by the glory of the Father, even so we also should walk in newness of life.

"Buried with him in baptism, wherein also we are raised with him, through faith in the power of God that raised him from the dead."—Col. ii. 12.

There is no need of mistake here. "Buried with him in immersion, wherein you also are raised with him," is good sense. But "buried with him in sprinkling," or "buried with him in pouring," is nonsense. It is not at all surprising that Luther, Calvin, Wesley, and a host of pedobaptist critics and commentators, should at once recognize the allusion to immersion in these passages. The only wonder is that any one should be so blinded by prejudice or so corrupted by party zeal, as to be unable to see it.

We will only add to these facts and reasonings, a brief historical statement. For all the facts stated below there is ample testimony; indeed, the candid and intelligent of whatever party, will rarely be found to dispute any of them.

1. The practice of the primitive church was immersion.

2. The practice in the time of the apostolic Fathers was immersion.

3. The practice of professed Christians until the fourteenth century, was immersion, except in the baptism of the sick. With Roman Catholics the change rests, not on scripture, but on church authority.

4. The practice of the Greek Church has always been immersion.

5. The Reformers, from Luther down, while frankly admitting that baptism was immersion, and that such was the practice of the primitive church, were led mainly by the influence of Calvin and his associates to substitute sprinkling for immersion, on the ground that the church had the right to change forms. It is the Roman Catholic doctrine of Church authority.

6. The substitution of sprinkling for immersion by the English Presbyterians, when the Directory for Worship was substituted for the rubrick of the Church of England, was accomplished by the casting vote of the Moderator of the Assembly—Dr. Lightfoot. The English ritual required that the child should be *dipped* in the font. This the Presbyterians cast aside, and declared that "sprinkling was not only lawful but sufficient," by a vote of 25 to 24.

7. While there is conscientious opposition to sprinkling and pouring, on the part of immersionists, on the ground of an invasion of divine authority by human commandments and traditions; and while there is continual doubt and fear on the part of thousands of pious persons about their sprinkling; *there is no doubt whatever in regard to immersion.* It is, without dispute, the only end of controversy on this question—the only baptism that all can accept; and should therefore be at once recognized by all who profess to follow the Lord Jesus, as the "one baptism" which meets all demands, ends all controversies, unites all believers, and buries the doubts of those to whom sprinkling and pouring have been a source of doubt and perplexity.

LETTER XVI.

The subject of Baptism.

Before we close our investigation of the question of Baptism, we must inquire as to its proper subjects. A very few paragraphs could have disposed of this whole question of baptism—mode, subjects, and design—had it not been for the protracted controversies of the past, and the confusion into which the minds of honest inquirers have been thrown. This necessitates a careful examination of the subject, in the light of the New Testament, as far removed as possible from the disputations of modern times. We say, *in the light of the* NEW TESTAMENT—because baptism is an ordinance of the New Testament, and not of the Old. This truth kept in mind, will rid the question of half its difficulties. It is well expressed in your old Standards; as, for instance, in the Westminster Confession, chap. xxviii.

"Baptism is a sacrament of the New Testament, *ordained by Jesus Christ*, not only for the solemn admission of the party baptized into the visible Church, but also to be unto him a sign and seal of the covenant of grace, of his ingrafting into Christ, of regeneration, of remission of sins, and of his giving up unto God through Jesus Christ, to walk in newness of life; which sacrament is, by *Christ's own appointment*, to be continued in his Church until the end of the world."

In the Exposition of the Confession, published by the Presbyterian Board of Publication, we have the following comment on the section which we have quoted:

"Baptism was not formerly appointed as a perpetual ordinance in the New Testament Church *until after the resurrection of Christ.*"

We are, then, in all consistency, relieved from the necessity for seeking in the Old Testament for authority for an ordinance—whether it regards action, subjects, or design—which was not instituted until long after the Old Testament canon was completed. We shall look in vain to Abraham or Moses for a knowledge of that which was not appointed "until after the resurrection of Christ." This accords entirely with what was written in our first letter touching the

New Testament superseding the Old, and of its having no force until after the death of the testator. It is in vain, then, the advocates of infant membership take us back to the Jewish Church, and beyond that to the time of Abraham. We are inquiring about an ordinance of the *New* Testament. That infant membership was established in one of the covenants made with Abraham (Gen. xvii.), and that it was incorporated into the law of Moses (John vii. 22, 23), is beyond dispute. But does it belong to the "New Testament Church" of which your Confession speaks? *That* is the question. The Kingdom of God, in its development, is compared to the growth of grain—"first the blade, then the ear, after that the full corn in the ear." Under the Gospel dispensation we look not for the *straw*, but for the "*ripe grain.*" Much belonged to the preparatory periods which perished when they expired. The "old bottles" held the "old wine," but Christ has taught us not to put the "*new* wine" of the Gospel into the "old bottles" of past dispensations. Matt. ix. 16, 17. There were "fleshly ordinances, imposed until the time of reformation" (Heb. ix. 10), which have lost all their sacredness. We must prove, then, that infant membership is found in the *new* covenant, or allow it to pass away with the effete ordinances of the Mosaic economy. Let us read the New Covenant and see if it warrants the idea of infant membership among its provisions.

> "But now he has obtained a more excellent ministry, inasmuch as he is the mediator of a better covenant, established on better promises. For if that first covenant had been faultless, then should no place have been sought for a second. For, finding fault with them, he saith, Behold the days come, saith the Lord, when I will make a new covenant with the house of Israel and with the house of Judah; *not according to the covenant* which I made with their fathers in the day when I took them by the hand to lead them out of the land of Egypt, because they continued not in my covenant, and I regarded them not, saith the Lord. For this is the covenant that I will make with the house of Israel after those days, saith the Lord:
>
> "I will put my laws into their mind, and write them in their hearts; and I will be to them a God, and they shall be to me a people; and they shall not teach every man his neighbor, and every man his brother, saying, know the Lord, for all shall know me from the least to the greatest; for I will be merciful to their unrighteousness, and their sins and their iniquities will I remember no more.
>
> "In that he said, A new covenant, he hath made the first old. Now that which decayeth and waxeth old is ready to vanish away."—*Heb.* viii. 6–13.

Now we think it cannot but strike the reader with great force that the marked contrasts between the Old and New Testaments, which is here sketched, involves the loss of infant membership.

The law of the old covenant was not adapted to the understanding, nor written in the hearts of its members. They came into the covenant by a fleshly birth, and were members of it before they had any understanding or affections. They were governed by external force, and they had an external law, "written and engraven on stones," and not in the heart. Its language was the language of stern authority, not addressed to the heart: "thou shalt," or, "thou shalt not"—enforced, not so much by gentle motives, enlisting the affections, as by the majesty and power revealed in fire, and darkness, and tempest, and earthquakes, and thundering utterances which led those who heard them to entreat that they might not hear them any more. Even Moses said, "I exceedingly fear and tremble." Heb. xii. 18–21. All this belonged legitimately to that stage in the development of the purposes of God. There was a fitness in infant membership in a national, politico-ecclesiastical dispensation; a fitness in circumcision—the fleshly mark by which a fleshly membership was attested; and a fitness in the stern authority of a law engraven in stones, to rule a fleshly community. But the *new* covenant is *spiritual*, not fleshly. Its blessings are spiritual blessings—forgiveness, adoption, and heirship of heavenly joys, not corn, and wine, and oil in a fruitful land. Hence its members are spiritual members, who enter it by a spiritual birth; and its laws are adapted to the understanding, and written on the heart, because men are born again through the quickening power of the truth and love which they receive into the heart, and can only become members of the covenant as they voluntarily and intelligently accept its obligations and its blessings. Its laws are not adapted to the understanding of an infant, nor written in the heart of a babe; therefore they do not and cannot belong to this covenant as they did in the former.

In the old covenant they did not know the Lord when they became members of it. They were born into it before they were capable of knowing. Hence they had to teach every man his neighbor and every man his brother to know the Lord, as they grew up to years of understanding.

But in the *new* covenant, they shall *not* thus teach, "*for all shall know me from the least to the greatest.*" Even the least in this covenant, whatever may be his weakness or ignorance in other matters, knows the Lord in his own blessed experience, as a God of mercy and love, because his sins are forgiven and the spirit of adoption fills his new-born soul with filial confidence and tone. He comes into the covenant, because he has learned of the mercy of God in Christ; and, renouncing his sins, and putting his trust in the Lamb of God who taketh away the sin of the world, he is "baptized into Christ"—is "born of water and of the Spirit" into the new covenant, and seizes the blood-sealed promise, "I will be merciful to your unrighteousness, and your sins and iniquities I will remember no more."

Clearly, then, infant membership is not only unrecognized in this covenant, but its genius, spirit, and promises are such as to exclude it entirely from the range of its provisions. Having learned the spiritual nature of the new covenant, and the inapplicability of its provisions to infants who have neither understanding nor heart, we proceed to inquire into the tenor of New Testament teaching, to learn whether it is in harmony with the genius and the requisitions of this covenant.

I.—THE TEACHING OF JOHN THE BAPTIST.

John was the harbinger of the Messiah. He "prepared the way of the Lord." In announcing his coming reign, and "making ready" a people for him, he necessarily foreshadowed the nature and character of the approaching kingdom. He baptized. *Whom* did he baptize? Those who came with the plea, "We have Abraham to our father?" Such a plea would be valid for circumcision, but it was not valid for baptism.

"Think not to say within yourselves, we have Abraham to our father; for I say unto you that God is able of these stones to raise up children to Abraham. And now also the axe is laid to the root of the trees. Every tree, therefore, which bringeth not forth good fruit is hewn down and cast into the fire."—Matt. iii. 9–10.

Here is an entire repudiation of hereditary privileges—of the doctrine of fleshly descent as the basis of religious rights. But this doctrine was the basis of infant membership and of covenant rights in the Jewish church. Infant membership and all covenant blessings growing out of fleshly descent, are, therefore, repudiated as not in harmony with the spirit and the aim of the coming kingdom of heaven. The axe, in John's hands, is laid at the roots of this tree of hereditary rights, and it is "cut down and cast into the fire." The doctrine of *personal responsibility* is now asserted as necessary to an appreciation of the kingdom of heaven. John will receive no one to baptism on the plea that he is a child of Abraham. Every one must repent *for himself*, and not claim the blessings of the kingdom on the virtues of another. His baptism was the "baptism of repentance for the remission of sins." Publicans and harlots who abandoned their sins, received this baptism; Pharisees and Sadducees who put in the plea that they were children of Abraham, were rejected. By this rule of personal repentance, infants were necessarily excluded.

II.—THE TEACHINGS OF JESUS.

1. His conversation with Nicodemus (John iii.), touching the nature of his kingdom, and the conditions of entrance, ought to settle this controversy forever.

"Jesus answered and said unto him, Verily, verily, I say unto thee, Except a man be born again (from above) he cannot see the kingdom of God.

"Nicodemus saith unto him, How can a man be born when he is old? Can he enter a second time into his mother's womb, and be born?

"Jesus answered, Verily, verily, I say unto thee, Except a man be born of water and of the Spirit, he can not enter into the kingdom of God. That which is born of flesh is flesh, and that which is born of the Spirit is spirit. Marvel not that I said unto thee, Ye must be born again."—John iii. 3–7.

Here the leading thought is, that the kingdom of God is *spiritual*, and can only be entered by those who are spiritually prepared for it. Nicodemus knew only of a fleshly birth. The law knew no other, as a condition of entrance into the covenant. *But Jesus repudiates fleshly descent. His* subjects must be born *from above*—of the Spirit as well as of water, or they cannot so much as see this spiritual kingdom. Now whatever difficulties may cluster about this teaching in John iii., it has no difficulties so far as our subject is concerned. No child has a right to membership in this kingdom by virtue of being born of certain parents. The ground must be taken of baptismal regenerationists—that the child in being baptized is really regenerated by the Spirit—or it must be admitted that they are excluded from the possibility of entrance into this kingdom. Baptism only admits those into the kingdom whom the Spirit of God has quickened into new life, renewing their minds and hearts. But the Spirit does not thus renew infants. They neither believe nor repent; they have neither love of God nor hate of sin; they bring no thought, desire, or emotion toward spiritual life; it is utter spiritual inanity. They cannot, therefore, *see* the kingdom of God. They have been born of flesh, and are fleshly. But they have not been born of the Spirit, and are not spiritual. Baptism, therefore, cannot admit them to the kingdom of God, for "except a man be born of water *and of the Spirit*, he cannot enter into the kingdom of God."

2. His mission is thus described by John:

"He came unto his own, and his own received him not; but as many as received him to them gave he power to become sons of God—even to them that believe on his name."—John i. 11–12.

Now, these were all members of the old covenant, and inherited all the blessings of that covenant. Yet to them, when they believed, he gave power to become sons of God. They were not children of God, therefore, by virtue of their infant membership in that old covenant. They had to be regenerated. They had to be born, "not of blood, nor of the will of the flesh, nor of the will of man, but of God." There is, therefore, a repudiation, by Christ, of all claims based on fleshly descent and infant membership. Membership in his family depends on being "born of God."

3. The apostolic commission is the fountain of authority, so far as Christian baptism is concerned. This reads:

"Go, teach all nations, baptizing them into the name of the Father, and of the Son, and of the Holy Spirit; teaching them to observe all things, whatsoever I have commanded you: and, lo, I am with you always, even unto the end of the world."—Matt. xxviii. 19, 20.

Or, as given by Mark:

"Go ye into all the world, and preach the Gospel to every creature. He that believeth and is baptized shall be saved; he that believeth not shall be damned."—Mark xvi. 15, 16.

Now, as the duties of the commissioned are limited by the language of their commission, so that they cannot rightfully go beyond what is there defined to be their duties, it is evident that the apostles had no authority to teach infant membership, or practice infant baptism, unless that authority is here conferred on them. Is it, then, found in this commission? They have here authority,

a. To preach the Gospel.

b. To baptize believers.

c. To teach the baptized all the duties of the Christian life.

But not one word about the baptism of infants. Then the apostles were without authority to baptize any but believers. Unless it is found here, if it could be proved that they baptized infants, it would simply prove that they transcended their authority. So forcibly is this felt, that pedobaptist commentators make a despairing effort to torture this commission into a meaning favorable to infant baptism. Thus, when it is said, "Go, *teach* all nations, baptizing them," *matheetüsate*, here rendered *teach*, is rendered *disciple:* "Go, disciple the nations baptizing them:" that is, disciple them, *by* baptizing them. Or as Dr. Shaff argues, Disciple the nations, *having baptized them.* He insists, with Meyer and Alford, that the *matheetüein* consists of two parts—the initiatory rite and the subsequent teaching; and that the process of discipleship is *from baptism to instruction — baptizontes* and *didaskontes* together covering the ground marked out by the previous *matheetüsate.* On this we remark:

1. This proves too much for them. For if this be the meaning of the commission, then the *first* duty of the apostles was to baptize the people, *whether infants or adults,* and afterward to teach them. But this is more than they are willing to admit. They must, then, abandon this style of criticism.

2. The verb *matheetüo* is found besides only in the following instances in the New Testament. "Every scribe *instructed* unto the kingdom of heaven." Matt. xxii. 15. "Who also himself was Jesus' *disciple.*" Matt. xxvii. 57. "And *had taught* many." Acts xvi. 21. Its use in these passages gives no countenance to such a construction.

3. *Matheetüsate* and *didaskontes,* both rendered *teach* in the common version of Matt. xxviii. 19, 20, are different terms. *Didasko* signifies *to teach, to admonish, to direct;* and

properly describes the didactical or preceptive instruction which is given in the school of Christ. While *matheetūo* is evidently used in the sense of *making a disciple*, or persuading him to enter the school of Christ. This is confirmed by the language of Mark, "Go into all the world, and *preach the Gospel* to every creature." They were, then, 1. To persuade men to become disciples by preaching the Gospel; 2. To baptize those whom they thus persuaded; 3. To teach the baptized the duties of the Christian life.

There is, therefore, no authority in the commission for baptizing infants, since the only rendering which would support such an idea would warrant and command the baptism of adults as well as infants, without knowledge, faith, or repentance.

It may be interesting, in closing the present Letter, to quote a few pedobaptist admissions on this text.

Baxter, often prejudiced, but always candid, says:

"As for those that say they are discipled by baptizing, and not before baptizing, they speak not the sense of the text; not that which is true or rational—else why should one be baptized more than another? This is not like some occasional historical mention of baptism; but it is the very commission of Christ to his apostles for preaching and baptizing; and purposely expresseth their several works in their several places and order. Their *first* task is, by teaching, to make disciples, which are by Mark called believers. The *second* work is to baptize them, whereto is annexed the promise of their salvation. The *third* work is, to teach them all other things which are afterward to be learned in the school of Christ. *To contemn this order is to renounce all rules of order;* for where can we expect to find it if not here? I profess, my conscience is fully satisfied from this text, that it is one kind of faith, even saving, that must go before baptism; and the profession whereof the minister must expect.—*Disput. to Right of Sacr.*, p. 91, 149, 150.

Even Calvin, in his commentary on this passage, is constrained to say:

"Because Christ requires teaching before baptizing, and will have believers only admitted to baptism, baptism does not seem rightly administered unless faith precede."

And the eminent Roman Catholic prelate, Kenrick, holds this language:

"But then it may be asked, On what authority can they be baptized? If the commission do not regard them, they are necessarily beyond its reach, and the attempt to baptize is an unauthorized measure. I care not to answer with some that the term rendered 'teach' may be understood of making disciples and initiating into Christ. Neither shall I allege, as a matter of mere inference, the divine command that each male infant, on the eighth day after his birth, should be circumcised and thus incorporated with the people of God: whence it is said the Apostles must have understood that infants should be admissible to the Christian rite which supersedes circumcision, especially inasmuch as the children of proselytes are said to have been washed with water when their parents were admitted to Jewish privileges. I do not at all allow that the Apostles were left to guess their Master's will from any circumstance; but I maintain that they were instructed by Him in the sacred functions intrusted to them, and were enlightened by the Holy Spirit that they might not err. The divine ordinance on this point, must be learned from their teaching and their acts, as recorded in Scripture; or, in the want of decisive evidence of this sort, from the teaching and practice of the church which they founded."—*Kenrick's Treatise on Baptism.*

This lands us in the native region of infant baptism—*Tradition.* In that lumber-house of ancient curiosities and monstrosities—that nest of all unclean and hateful superstitions, this perversion of the truth may be found in association with scores of corrupt and corrupting innovations—the offspring of the spirit of apostacy.

III. *The Teaching and Practice of the Apostles.*

1. We have already written so fully of the significance of the events recorded in Acts ii., when the will of our Lord and Savior was opened and announced by the executors—when the kingdom was established, and its laws and ordinances for the first time authoritatively announced, that we will not need to repeat it here. Let us see if, at this important epoch, when the gates of the kingdom were unlocked by the apostle Peter, infants entered in. We find, on examination, that the order of the commission is scrupulously observed. *a.* They preached the Gospel, that men might believe. *b.* They called on believers to repent and be baptized. *c.* "*Then they that gladly received the word were baptized.*" No infants admitted here. Will you say that, having been circumcised, there was no need to practice a rite which came in the room of cir-

cumcision? We answer, all the male adults who were baptized had previously been circumcised; and if baptism came in the room of circumcision, there was no need of any of them being baptized!

2. The subsequent history of apostolic labors is all in harmony with this. The Samaritans, when they believed, "were baptized, both men and women." Acts viii. 12. At the house of Cornelius, "the Holy Spirit fell *on all them which heard the word.*" They spoke in various languages, and magnified God. "*Then*, said Peter, Can any man forbid water, that these should not be baptized who have received the Holy Spirit as well as we?" Acts x. 45–47. This is one of the *household* baptisms! At Antioch "a great number *believed* and turned to the Lord. Acts xi. 21. At Antioch in Pisidia, "as many as were ordained to eternal life *believed*." Acts xiii. 48. At Iconium, "a great multitude both of the Jews and also of the Greeks, *believed*." Acts xiv. 1. When Paul and Barnabas returned from an extensive missionary tour, "they rehearsed all that God had done with them, and how He had opened *the door of faith* to the Gentiles." Acts xiv. 27. The jailor believed in God, *with all his house*, and believing, they were baptized. Acts xvi. 30–34. At Corinth, "Crispus, the chief ruler of the synagogue, believed on the Lord *with all his house;* and many of the Corinthians, hearing, believed,

and were baptized." Acts xviii. 8. This is the uniform current of testimony through the Acts of Apostles. Faith always preceded baptism. Even in the cases of households, it was households of believers.

3. In preaching and teaching, the apostles speak of baptism always in such associations and with such qualifications as to make their language entirely inapplicable to infants.

In the commission it is associated with faith; on the day of Pentecost, with repentance; in Samaria, it is *men and women* that are baptized after believing; those are baptized who are "dead to sin," and who rise to "newness of life;" Rom. vi. 2–4; if the church is cleansed by the washing of water, it is added, "*through the word;*" Eph. v. 26; if we are saved by the washing of regeneration, it is immediately added, "and renewing of the Holy Spirit;" Titus iii. 5; if our bodies are washed with pure water, in immediate connection with it, the heart is sprinkled from an evil conscience; Heb. x. 22; and if baptism is spoken of as saving us, the salvation is defined to be "the answer of a good conscience toward God." 1 Pet. iii. 21. It is impossible to apply such language as is always found associated with baptism, to infants. It is ever an act of faith.

It only remains that we notice some of the more plausible arguments for infant membership. Not having much space left, we will pay attention to a few of the strongest; for if these are unsound, the feebler ones are unworthy of attention.

1. It is argued that infant membership is older than the Jewish covenant, and did not therefore perish with it. It goes back to Abraham's time (Gen. xvii.), and as the seal of spiritual blessings, is not interfered with by the abrogation of the law of Moses.

To this we reply—

a. Although it began before the law, it was established in anticipation of the law, was incorporated with the law, and for 1,500 years rested on the authority of the law, and of that only. (See John vii. 22, 23.) The authority of patriarchal times gave way to the authority of Moses; and when the authority of Moses, as lawgiver, ceased, circumcision necessarily ceased with it, unless re-enacted by the new Lawgiver, Christ Jesus.

b. Circumcision did not seal spiritual blessings to the members of that covenant. To Abraham, individually, it was a seal of the righteousness of the faith which he had before he was circumcised (Rom. iv. 11), but it was this to none others, either adults or infants, to whom it was administered. The covenant of circumcision secured the land of Canaan, divine protection in that inheritance, and abundance of earthly good. The spiritual blessings covenanted to Abraham were embraced in another covenant (see Gen. xii.), which was confirmed, not by circumcision, but by the oath of God. Compare Gen. xii. 1–3, and xxii. 15–18, with Gal. iii. 8, 17, and Heb. vi. 13–18. The Gospel engrosses the covenant of Gen. xii., and confers its blessings, through Christ, on the children of faith, even as the law engrossed the covenant of Gen. xvii., and conferred its blessings on the children of the flesh.

2. Jesus said, "Suffer little children to come to me, and forbid them not, for of such is the kingdom of heaven." Matt. xix. 14.

Answer.—*Such* is a term of comparison. Of *such* is the kingdom, does not mean, of *these* is the kingdom, but of those who are like these in certain particulars. Matt. xviii. 1–5 furnishes an illustration. A little child was set in the midst of the disciples when they were contending about who should be greatest, and they were told, "Whosoever shall *humble* himself *as this little child*, the same is greatest in the kingdom of heaven." But Christ's "little ones" are *believers.* "Whoso shall offend one of these little ones *that believe in me*," etc. Matt. xviii. 6.

Moreover, Christ did not *baptize* these children, nor take them into church relations. He *blessed* them. As neither baptism nor church membership is in the *premises*, neither of them can logically be in the *conclusion.*

3. "For the unbelieving husband is sanctified by the wife, and the unbelieving wife is sanctified by the husband; else were your children unclean, but now are they holy." 1 Cor. vii. 14. It is argued that the child of a believing parent is "holy" and therefore entitled to church membership.

Answer.—The unbelieving husband or wife is "holy," or "sanctified," in the same sense and in the same way. Hence if this proves that the children have a right to church membership on the faith of the parent, it proves that the unbelieving husband or wife has also a right to church membership, on precisely the same ground! This proves too much—therefore, nothing.

Paul argues with the members of the Corinthian Church who insisted that any of their number who were married to heathen partners should dissolve that relationship, in this style: "The unbelieving husband or wife sustains the same relation to their Christian partners that your children sustain to you. Your children are unbelievers, and it is yet lawful for you to preserve your relationship to them unbroken. Even so may the believing wife preserve unbroken her relationship to an unbelieving husband." Observe, he says "*your* children," not "*their* children;" thus proving that these children of Christians sustained the same relation to them that an unbelieving husband did to a believing wife. Most evidently, then, these children were not in church relationship.

But we have furnished specimens enough to show how weak and fallacious are these objections.

It only remains to say that infant membership corrupts the purity of the church.

1. It loads unregenerate natures with the responsibilities of religious life, without their own consent.

2. It breaks down, to the extent of its prevalence, the distinction between the church and the world. If it were to prevail, as it does in some instances, over a whole nation, the distinction between the church and the world is utterly lost, and all the crimes of the nation are the crimes of the church. It becomes an essential part of the machinery for uniting Church and State, and thus aids in superinducing the mischiefs and outrages ever consequent on such union.

It does not and cannot belong to that pure spiritual institution which its Founder declared to be "not of this world."

As you have revealed some rationalistic sympathies, allow me to close what I have to say on the whole subject of baptism by a quotation from *Ecce Homo*, whose author, whether a Rationalist or not, is evidently viewing the mission of Jesus from the Rationalist's stand-point:

"When we consider the great contempt which Christ constantly expressed for forms and ceremonies, and in particular for those 'washings' which were usual among the Pharisees, we are prepared to find Him readily acceding to the request of Nicodemus, instead of which he shut the petitioner's mouth by an abrupt declaration that there was no way into the Theocracy but through baptism. The kingdom of God, he insisted, though it had no locality, and no separation from the secular states of mankind; though it had no law-courts, no lictors, and no fasces, was yet a true state. Men were not to make a light thing of entering it, to give their names to the Founder at a secret interview, and immediately return to their accustomed places of resort, and take up the routine of secular life where it had been left. Those who would enroll themselves among the citizens of it, were to understand that they began their life anew, as truly as if they had been born again. And lest the Divine Society, in its contempt for material boundaries, and for the distinctness which is given by unity of place, should lose its distinctness altogether, and degenerate into a theory, or a sentiment, or a devout imagination, the initiatory rite of baptism, with its publicity and formality, was pronounced as indispensable to membership as that spiritual inspiration which is membership itself. * * * The water in which they were bathed washed away from them the whole unhallowed and unprofitable past; they rose out of it new men into a new world, and felt as though death were behind them, and they had been born again into a higher state."

This is not just the language in which we would choose to express our own convictions; but we give it to show how, apart from all partisan leanings, and even with a daring purpose that respects no prejudices of the past, a candid mind is compelled to recognize the significance and necessity of this ordinance.

LETTER XVII.

Privileges, Duties, Enjoyments, and Destiny of the Christian.

In concluding this series of Letters, it is proper to say something of the *promises* of the Gospel—the *relations* into which it brings us—and the *obligations* which we assume in entering into these relations. These we must very briefly sketch, as the limits of our concluding epistle compel brevity.

The order of the Gospel is—1. Faith. 2. Obedience. 3. Enjoyment of Gospel blessings. 4. A Christian life. 5. A destiny of immortality. We have spoken of Faith and Obedience. It remains to speak of the enjoyments of the Christian, and the life he is to live.

Concerning the promises, we notice,

1.—*The forgiveness of sins.*—In the fullest sense, the baptized believer receives the forgiveness of all past sins; in a sense so ample that it is called *justification*—that is, he is accepted in Christ, and through the atonement of the Lamb of God, as if he had never sinned at all. His sins are "covered." His faith in the atoning sacrifice is counted to him for righteousness. The covenant promise is sealed to him: "I will be merciful to your unrighteousness, and your sins and iniquities I will remember no more." In the law there was a remembrance of sins made every year. (Lev. xvi.) In the Gospel it is an "everlasting righteousness"—a "perfect redemption."

2.—*Adoption.*—The justified believer is taken into the family of God—privilege is given to him to become a child of God; the highest rank to which a created being can be elevated. Divine protection, guidance and support are assured to him—not to save him from the sorrows and tribulations of mortal life, but—to lead him safely through all these to the attainment of everlasting life. The special providence of God is not for ease, wealth, or safety here, but that all things may work together for the *final* good—the "endless life."

3.—*The Holy Spirit.*—Along with the remission of sins, the Gospel promises "the gift of the Holy Spirit." Acts ii. 38. The Spirit was to abide "for ever." By the spirit of adoption, sent forth into the hearts of the children, they were to be enabled, with filial reverence and trust, to look up to heaven and cry, Abba, Father. Gal. iv. 6. The love of God was to be shed abroad in their hearts by the Holy Spirit given to them. Rom. v. 5. They were to be strengthened with might by the Spirit in the inner man. Eph. iii. 16. Paul expressed confidence that his trials would contribute to his salvation through the prayers of his brethren and the supply of the Spirit of Jesus Christ. Phil. i. 19. Our Lord taught his disciples to pray for the Spirit. Luke xv. 13.

The Spirit was the *seal* of the promises, the *earnest* of the future inheritance (Eph. i. 13, 14), and the *guest* alike of the individual believer and of the church of God. Rom. viii. 11; 1 Cor. vi. 19; Eph. ii. 22. So that "the grace of our Lord Jesus Christ" in the forgiveness of sins, the "love of God" in blessed Fatherhood, and "the communion of the Holy Spirit" as the joint heritage of all the children of God, are the perpetual benediction on the household of faith. 2 Cor. xiii. 14.

These are certainly "exceedingly great and precious promises, whereby we are made partakers of the divine nature having escaped from the corruption that is in the world through lust." 2 Pet. i. 4.

It will be seen at a glance that in order to the fulfillment of these promises, the believer is brought into new relations. He is baptized "*into* the name of the Father, and of the Son, and of the Holy Spirit." Matt. xxviii. 19. His baptism is *in the name*, or by the authority of the Lord Jesus; but *into* the name of Father, Son and Holy Spirit; for he is thus brought into new relations to these. The Father is now *his* Father; the Son is *his* kinsman Redeemer; the Holy Spirit is *his* Sanctifier. As a result, his relations are changed to the whole universe. Angels are his ministering servants; Christians are his brethren; bad men and demons are his enemies. He is a member of the

Church of God; a child in the divine family; a fellow-citizen with the saints in the kingdom of God; an heir of the eternal inheritance. He *has* come to Mount Zion, and to the city of the living God, the heavenly Jerusalem, and to an innumerable company of angels, to the general assembly and church of the first-born who are written in heaven, and to God, the judge of all, and to the spirits of just men made perfect, and to Jesus the mediator of the new covenant, and to the blood and sprinkling." Heb. xii. 22–24. In new and blessed relationships he stands affiliated with all that is pure and bright and grand in the whole universe—heir of all things—and possesses, in the "righteousness, peace, and joy" of his new-born soul the "earnest of the inheritance." Though he be "the least in the kingdom," he is "greater than John the Baptist"—for the Messiah whom John only pointed out is *his* brother, the Holy Spirit of which John prophesied is *his* in possession, the kingdom which John proclaimed as near, he possesses in its trinity of blessings—"righteousness and peace and joy in the Holy Spirit," and the official rank of John as the harbinger of the Messiah, is far transcended by the personal rank of the lowliest Christian as a child of God.

Out of these pure and exalted relationships spring certain obligations. He owes duties to God, to the church, and to the world. As a child, he owes reverence, love and obedience to his Father. As a redeemed man, he owes all the powers of his ransomed nature to Him who has paid the ransom. As a temple of the Holy Spirit, he owes to this divine Guest a clean and loving heart—an upright and holy life. As a brother, he owes love and service to all the divine family. As a man, he owes good will and philanthropy to all his kind. He is to live "soberly, righteously, and godly in the present world:" *soberly*, in the control of his own nature; *righteously*, in discharging all his duties to his fellows; *godly*, in the cultivation of pious gratitude and reverence toward God. In a word, he is to be a follower of Christ.

To aid him in this great work of building up a true character, he has,

1. The word of grace.
2. The throne of grace.
3. The Spirit of grace.

The word of grace instructs him: the throne of grace supplies pardon when he is sinful, shelter when he is in danger, and strength when he is weary; the Spirit of grace abides in him as a "well of water springing up into everlasting life:" a fountain of divine strength, comfort and peace. We may add to all these *the fellowship of saints*—the sympathy of kindred hearts, and all the light and love ministered by the ordinances of the church of God. So that he is enriched with all spiritual blessings in heavenly relationships through Christ Jesus, and is abundantly furnished unto all good works.

There is everything pure and nothing carnal or sensual, in the blessings with which he is enriched; every thing noble and exalted, and nothing mean or unworthy in the relationships into which he comes; every thing just and good and nothing mean or dishonorable in the life to which he is called.

And the *end* of all this is—"eternal life through Jesus Christ our Lord." His education in the church militant fits him for a kingly destiny in the church triumphant. His spirit is to be perfectly purified, and his body transcendently glorified; so that a purified spirit in a glorified body, robed in righteousness, crowned with fadeless glory, filled with the treasures of immortal blessedness, and invested with high dominion, will reign in fadeless grandeur, and rejoice in deathless love.

But here we pause. We can command no language to express, as we can summon no powers adequate to conceive the immortal honors, the peerless dignities, the ineffable felicities, the unimaginable glories of a glorified man. "Exceedingly abundant beyond all that we can ask or think" will be the treasures of the grace of God to his redeemed children. We can only rise on the stepping stones of our Christian experience here in life and in death; and as we slake our thirst at the fountain of His mercy here, and share the "peace that passeth all understanding," say in rapturous anticipation—

> "If such the sweetness of the *streams*,
> What must the *fountain* be,
> Where saints and angels draw their bliss
> Immediately from thee!"

We must close. Will you, my dear sir, give to all these unfoldings of the plan of salvation the attention which their importance demands? This theme transcends all others in real value. The best riches and honors and pleasures of earth are but baubles in comparison with these spiritual and eternal treasures. If you turn away from Christ, you turn from the only Sun of Righteousness to endless night. If you follow the teachings of modern Rationalism they will lead you a sorry chase through bog and mire, and land you in hopeless despondency. Its daring speculations attract more than they instruct, and shatter faith without strengthening reason. They may rob you of Christ, but they have none other to supply his place for guidance here or life hereafter; and while you may be for a moment exultant as they exalt you to a pinnacle of pride and self-sufficiency, it will only be to fall from your position into dust and ashes, and perish without hope. Your old theology cannot satisfy your cravings.

It is too subtle, too dogmatic, and too inconsistent. You have no right to submit to the dictation of a human creed which the world and the church have outgrown. The word of God alone is sure, and abideth forever. Come to Jesus. Sit at His feet. Take His yoke on you, and learn of Him, and you will find rest to your soul. His yoke is easy. His burden is light. He is the Way, the Truth, the Life. Blessed are all they that put their trust in Him.

www.ingramcontent.com/pod-product-compliance
Lightning Source LLC
LaVergne TN
LVHW021403110826
845150LV00007B/1760

* 9 7 8 1 4 2 5 5 1 2 3 6 1 *